MARIANNE WILLIAMSON

HEALING
THE
SOUL
OF
AMERICA

Reclaiming Our Voices
as Spiritual Citizens

A TOUCHSTONE BOOK
PUBLISHED BY SIMON & SCHUSTER

TOUCHSTONE
Rockefeller Center
1230 Avenue of the Americas
New York, NY 10020

Copyright © 1997, 2000 by Marianne Williamson
All rights reserved,
including the right of reproduction
in whole or in part in any form.

First Touchstone Edition 2000

Touchstone and colophon are registered trademarks
of Simon & Schuster, Inc.

Designed by Songhee Kim

Manufactured in the United States of America

3   5   7   9   10   8   6   4   2

Library of Congress Cataloging-in-Publication Data

Williamson, Marianne, 1952–
Healing the soul of America : reclaiming our voices as spiritual citizens /
Marianne Williamson. — 1st Touchstone ed.
p.   cm.
Rev. ed. of: The healing of America. c1997.
Includes bibliographical references and index.
1. United States—Religion.   2. Spirituality—United States.   3. Religion and
culture—United States.   4. Religion and politics—United States.
I. Williamson, Marianne, 1952– Healing of America.   II. Title.
BL2525.W495   1999
973—dc21   99-35876
                                        CIP
ISBN 0-684-84270-X
ISBN 0-684-84622-5 (Pbk)

This is a revised edition of *The Healing of America.*

For Al Lowman,
with thanks and love

CONTENTS

PREFACE

M A N Y people are going around today saying, "In any situation, I just ask myself, 'What would Buddha, or Jesus, do? What would the Torah tell me to do, or the Koran, or the New Testament?' " Thinking about such things is a perfect test, reading the news today. Would Jesus, if he were a citizen of the richest nation on earth, choose to feed the poor or fatten the rich? It's certainly an interesting question.

All of us are better off when contemplation of holy principles is at the center of our lives. But it is in actually *applying* those principles that we forge the marriage between heaven and earth, while merely dwelling on principle falls short of the human effort needed to carry out God's will. Just as we need the light of the sun—but looking straight into it can blind us—looking straight into the inner light can begin to blind us as well.

There is a point in everyone's spiritual journey where, if you are not careful, the search for self-awareness can turn into self-preoccupation. There is a fine line, at times, between self-exploration and narcissism. One way to see how we're doing is to measure the fun factor: spiritual growth that's too much fun all the time usually isn't growth at all. Anything that has become too comfortable cannot ultimately be comforting. The universe is invested in our healing, and healing is a fierce, transformative fire.

It is the product of human willingness to change, and change is often hard.

For years, I thought I only had to heal myself, and the world would take care of itself. Clearly we must work on healing our own neuroses in order to become effective healers. But then, having worked on our own issues a while, another question begs for an answer: how healed can we ultimately become while the social systems in which we live and move, and have our earthly being, remain sick?

Years ago, we realized that people's psychology is intimately bound up with the psychology of their family units. Today, it is very clear that the family, too, dwells within a larger psychological system. It's not just our childhoods or families whose dysfunctions influence us; our education system, government, and business structures are often dysfunctional as well, and in a manner that affects us all. None of us lives in isolation anymore, from anyone or anything.

The principles that apply to our personal healing apply as well to the healing of the larger world. First, all healing principles are universal because they come from God. And second, there actually *is* no objective outer world, for what's out there is merely a projection of what's in our minds. The laws of consciousness apply to everything. Anything, when truly seen for what it is and surrendered to the higher mind, begins to self-correct. But what is *not* looked at is doomed to eternal re-enactment, for an individual or for a nation.

Politics, ideally, is a context for the care of the public good. The word *politics* comes from an ancient Greek root *politeia*, meaning not "of the government," but rather "gathering of citizens." *The source of power in America is not the government; the source of power is us.* And millions of us, citizens of the United States, have begun to see life in a less mechanistic, more enlightened way. The consciousness revolution has already transformed both mainstream medicine and business: Harvard Medical School has hosted symposiums on the role of spirituality and healing in medicine, and highly paid corporate consultants call on business executives to turn their workplaces into "sanctuaries for the soul." Government is the only major American institution that doesn't yet seem to have heard that the world has unalterably changed.

There are new ideas on the world's horizon, as different from the twentieth-century worldview as the twentieth century was different from the nineteenth century. We are ready to apply principles of healing and recovery, not just to our bodies, not just to our relationships, but to every aspect of life.

World conditions challenge us to look beyond the status quo for responses to the pain of our times. We look to powers within as well as to powers without. A new, spiritually based social activism is beginning to assert itself. It stems not from hating what is wrong and trying to fight it, but from loving what could be and making the commitment to bring it forth. A nonviolent political dynamic is once again emerging, and it is a beacon of light at the dawn of the twenty-first century. Its goal, as in the words of Martin Luther King, Jr., is "the establishment of the beloved community." Nothing less will heal our hearts and nothing less will heal the world.

It is a task of our generation to recreate the American *politeia*, to awaken from our culture of distraction and re-engage the process of democracy with soulfulness and hope. Yes, we see there are problems in the world. But we believe in a universal force that, when activated by the human heart, has the power to make all things right. Such is the divine authority of love: to renew the heart, renew the nations, and ultimately, renew the world.

Amen.

INTRODUCTION

When a country obtains great power,
it becomes like the sea:
all streams run downward into it.
The more powerful it grows,
the greater the need for humility.
Humility means trusting the Tao,
thus never needing to be defensive.

A great nation is like a great man:
When he makes a mistake, he realizes it.
Having realized it, he admits it.
Having admitted it, he corrects it.
He considers those who point out his faults
as his most benevolent teachers.
He thinks of his enemy
as the shadow that he himself casts.

If a nation is centered in the Tao,
if it nourishes its own people
and doesn't meddle in the affairs of others,
it will be a light to all nations in the world.
　　　　　—LAO TZU, *TAO TE CHING*
　　　(translated by Stephen Mitchell)

ACCORDING to ancient Chinese philosophy, the forces of yin and yang create the balance of the universe. They manifest as night and day, darkness and light, feminine and masculine, inner and outer, heart and head. They balance, border, and complete each other, forming together a unified whole.

Understanding this dynamic affords us a deeper awareness of the rhythms underlying all things. Yin and yang emanate from a primordial Oneness that the Chinese call the Tao, a mystical underpinning to all worldly events. This Oneness, which is the field from whence all possibilities flow, constantly choreographs a dancing universe. The dual forces of the phenomenal world make passionate moves at every turn. Where there is yin, yang finds it; where there is yang, yin awaits. This dance creates the drama of human existence, the metaphysical engine that makes the world go round.

This book is about the yin and yang of American history: the miraculous combination of vision and politics that gave rise to our beginnings, their ultimate rending at the hands of unbridled human passion, and the current yearning of the American heart to put them back together.

Our Founders embodied the ideals of an extraordinary moment in time, and with the success of the American Revolution they created one of the miracles of modern history. Heirs to the European Age of Enlightenment—a movement proclaiming the inherent goodness of man—our Founders expressed their philosophical vision in the Declaration of Independence and their political genius in the U.S. Constitution. Their balance of intellectual brilliance with personal courage, philosophical vision with political acumen, and mature serenity with revolutionary fervor created a doorway in a seemingly impenetrable wall of history. The Western world was stuck, and they unstuck it.

The founding of the United States was a dramatic repudiation of the *ancien regime*—a social structure that dominated all of Europe for centuries, placing power in the hands of monarchs and aristocracy, and relegating the masses to serfdom and servitude. A worldview so entrenched as to leave the common masses of humanity little hope of rising above the station in life into which they had been born was abolished forever by a group of young Americans who stood up to what was then the most powerful military force in the world and said, "No. We have a better idea." They were young and rebellious and—like all revolutionaries— in the eyes of some, quite out of their minds. Their audacity is part of our national heritage.

Today, most Americans are too cynical, or tired, or both, to even approximate our Founders' courageous repudiation of injustice. Where they claimed their rights to assert power, we routinely countenance the diminution of our own. Looking at what they did to broaden their freedom helps inspire us to reinvigorate ours.

Our Founders' primary genius was to rethink political power. They transformed political authority from a governmental source to a citizen source, in keeping with the exaltation of individual goodness so prevalent during the Age of the Enlightenment. American democracy is a transcendent notion, positing that power flows not from without but from within. It was not to be the wealth or power of one's outer circumstances, but the spirit of intelligent goodness which resides inside us all that was entrusted with the authority to rule this nation.

This was a radical thought then and it is a radical thought now. It is radical, yet it is fragile. You can't just set yourself up as a democracy, and that's it. A chain depends on every link. Every generation must relearn and recommit to the foundations of democracy, as they are something that can never ever be taken for granted. The strength of the democratic concept has not gone away—but neither have the forces of narrow-mindedness, dominance, and fear that would threaten its existence.

After our extraordinary beginnings in a burst of democratic fervor, we turned our attention to other matters. Within a hundred years of our founding, by the latter part of the nineteenth century, the Industrial Revolution raged throughout Europe and the United States. Railroads, electricity, and factory production were the order of the day; scientific experimentation and technological prowess came to embellish our dreams and define our ambitions. As this rush of industrial expansion unfolded, the yang of human assertion and physical manifestation was extraordinary. It's easy to see how the Western mind became obsessed with America's material success.

Yet we lost something very precious as the yin of greater wisdom and understanding was subtly pushed to the side. Intoxicated by technological possibilities, we slowly lost our focus on the light at the center of everything. By the beginning of the twentieth century—despite the valiant efforts of some of our greatest poets and philosophers—attention to our souls had been marginalized by a materialistic focus sweeping across the plains of America's consciousness like a windstorm that wouldn't stop.

Money began to replace justice as our highest ambition, and the authoritarian business models of the Industrial Age came to replace democracy as the main organizing principle of American society. The elements of higher truth that so imbued our founding—the stunning declaration that all men are created equal and should share equal rights to life, liberty, and the pursuit of happiness—were insidiously exiled to the corners of the American mind. They remained in our documents but began a slow and tortured exit from our hearts.

The very tyrannies from which we had fought to be free would reappear among us, and this time we were the oppressors as well as the oppressed. With every generation—including our own—we've waged a fiery personal and political contest between our most noble and our basest thoughts. Which would control the destiny of this nation?

We expanded our physical territory and our commitment to freedom, applying our highest ideals as we abolished slavery, gave women the right to vote, banned child labor, and in many other ways remained true to the goal of an expanding democracy. Had the Industrial Revolution, with its gargantuan focus on material power, not occurred, then the magnificence of our original ideals might have continued to pull us upward and out of the devolutionary lure of history. But it did occur, and while it allowed the world phenomenal opportunity for the eradication of material suffering, it also clearly fostered our spiritual forgetfulness. Material progress become an American god.

To look in our national mirror is to see both glory and shame. Born of a stunning assertion of the human spirit in the face of tyranny, we then built a nation on the blood of Native Americans and slaves from Africa. We endured the horrors of a Civil War, heroically fought two World Wars, brilliantly helped defeat Hitler—and then imperialistically devastated Vietnam. We are blessed with more money and more technological resources than any other nation of the world, yet we give only six-tenths of 1 percent of our budget away to nations less fortunate than we. We are a nation that loves to say how much we love our children, yet children are less well cared for in America than in any of our industrialized counterparts.

America has always been a land of contradictions. We have been both slaveowner and abolitionist, conscienceless industrialist and labor reformer, corporate polluter and world-class environmentalist. Sometimes we have embodied the most brutish attitudes and at other times, in Lincoln's words, "the angels of our better nature." But no matter what any of us have chosen to manifest at any particular time, the American ideal as established by our founding documents remains the same: the expression of humanity at its most free and creative and just. That is the point and purpose of this country as represented on the Great Seal of the United States. This mystical seal, designed by Franklin, Adams, and Washington, pictures the capstone returned to the Great Pyramid at Giza, a Masonic symbol for wisdom. The eye of Horus, representing humanity's higher mind, dazzlingly proclaims that here we will achieve *Novus Ordo Seclorum,* a "new order of the ages," the age of universal brotherhood. That thought, regardless of how corrupted and bastardized it has been at various points in our history, remains our spiritual and political mission. The power of the ideal continues to shine like a beacon for all Americans, exhorting us to become what we originally committed to becoming.

Clearly, our original principles of human justice and freedom—that here, mankind would find sanctuary from the institutionalized tyrannies of the world—have never been fully manifest, but that does not mean that we are bad or even hypocritical. It means only that we are a nation still in the throes of a greater becoming. Our Founders began a process that every generation is challenged to further. A nation is not a *thing* so much as a process; we're not a particle, but a wave.

The Declaration of Independence, the Constitution, the Bill of Rights, the Emancipation Proclamation, the Gettysburg Address, Kennedy's Inaugural Address, King's Letter from a Birmingham Jail—these are like ancient tablets on which are inscribed our fundamental yearnings and highest hopes. At the same time, slavery, the Trail of Tears, the Vietnam War, systemic racism and economic injustice, official hypocrisy, violence, and exalted militarism form a dark and seemingly impenetrable forcefield acting like a barrier before our hearts, keeping our hands from being able to grasp those tablets to our chests. It is the task of our generation to break through the wall before us, to atone for our errors and reactivate our commitment to the promulgation of our strengths. It is not just that we need our sacred tablets; our sacred tablets, to be living truths, need us.

There is so much injustice in America today, yet such conspiracy not to discuss it; there is so much suffering, yet so much deflection lest we notice. Greed is considered legitimate now, while brotherly love is not.

Thirty-six million people—including a fifth of America's children—live in poverty in the richest nation of the world. That is a number equal to every man, woman, and child in the largest twenty-five cities in America. Millions of children go to school each day in buildings that do not meet minimum safety codes, do not have enough school supplies, or do not even have working toilets. One hundred thousand of them take guns to school each day. Millions more are abandoned, neglected, abused. We now imprison more people—six times more than either Russia or China—than any other nation on earth, and the vast majority of our prisoners are people of color. As is usually the case when a nation has a very high percentage of its citizens behind bars, a small portion of our population controls the vast majority of our wealth. Today, we are not so much doing well at manifesting our highest ideals as we are encased in a neurotic cultural denial regarding the depth of their violation.

Do we not know these things, or are we merely desensitized to the facts? What happened to us that we have become so complacent? Why are we not *demanding* that these situations be ameliorated? While we politically broke free of serfdom over two hundred years ago, perhaps we have not yet achieved the psychological and spiritual and emotional conditions necessary to *sustain* our freedoms. The needs of our business institutions are consistently placed before the needs of our people, and the trend is getting worse instead of better. Corporations have become a new aristocracy, while the average American is a new brand of serf. The difference now is that it is possible to buy one's way into the aristocracy; that, however, is a far cry from removing the institution.

We have exported democracy around the world, while at home we could clearly use a democratic renewal. From the FDIC's trying to pass "Know Your Customer" laws requiring banks to report to the government every citizen's private financial transactions, to industrial agricultural giants practically forcing genetically engineered food into our food supply and trying to outlaw efforts by anyone to let us know, there is a scepter of big brother in the air, growing uglier every day. What happened to Americans, that we have become so easy to seduce with a tax cut here or distract with a sex scandal there? What happened that we are willing to place the good of corporations before the good of our children, that we have been willing to countenance the corruption of our political system by the dominance of corporate wealth? What happened to the "spirit of rebellion" without which, according to Thomas Jefferson, democracy cannot survive? We, the citizens of the freest, most powerful nation on earth, have become oddly disempowered. Short-term economic gain has become so solidly our bottom line that scarcely anyone dares question the moral damage this is doing to the American soul.

Independent thought is a rebellious act, not always appreciated by one's environment. Throughout human history—from Jesus to Galileo to the Founders of the United States to Martin Luther King, Jr.—the status quo has never embraced the harbingers of its demise. Our nation, as we have seen, was literally created out of the rebellion against an entrenched and tyrannous status quo. Today's average American, however, is more apt to rebel against a tennis shoe not coming in the right color than against the slow erosion of our democratic freedoms.

It is always inspiring to bear witness to great spirits who preceded us, who lived as we do in both exciting and difficult times, and whose lives bore witness to the hunger for some transcendent good. There have been those in history who personified perfectly, or nearly so, the balance of soul and political intelligence necessary to right the wrongs of history. From our Founders, to Lincoln, to Mahatma Gandhi, to Martin Luther King, Jr., there are those that humanity can point to and say, "There, they got it right." They, like us, did not have perfect childhoods or face simple problems. They, too, had obstacles to their full becoming. Their significance is all the greater because they did.

Our Founders had a job to do: to win freedom from the English and forge for the United States our own political identity. Lincoln had a job to do: to preserve the Union and make it a nation worth fighting for. Gandhi had a job to do: to lead a nonviolent crusade for India's independence. Dr. King had a job to do: to lead the struggle for American civil rights. These people didn't whine; they acted. They didn't give in to despair; they created revolutions. They didn't curse the darkness; they became the light—passionately intelligent people in service to the job at hand. They put aside their childish inclinations and served a process larger than themselves. They were not without pain, nor were they perfect people—any more than we are perfect—when they heard and responded to the call of history. They answered the plea for democracy and justice made throughout the ages, and having answered it, were given all the strength they needed to bring forth the resurrection of good. These were not geniuses who just happened to care about the human race; they were people who cared passionately about the human race, and out of that passion their genius emerged.

Love is its own brand of genius. Our only true enemy is neither people or institutions, but fear-laden thoughts that cling to our insides and sap us of our strength. Yet love casts out fear, the way light casts out darkness. Our greatest political power, now, is to fear nothing and love everything; then all things will heal. Love is the only power powerful enough to lift the chains of bondage off the human race and cast them off for good. When the material world has been won by the opponent, go otherworldly to find your victory.

The words of Abraham Lincoln, in his 1862 Annual Message, echo to us now: "Fellow citizens, we cannot escape history. We . . . will be remembered in spite of ourselves. No personal significance or insignificance can spare one or another of us. The fiery trial through which we pass will light us down in honor or dishonor to the last generation. . . . We shall nobly save or meanly lose the last, best hope of earth."

Americans have the yang; it's time to reclaim the yin. We have the intelligence; it's time to retrieve our souls. We have a political democracy still; it's time to reclaim our commitment to keeping it, and live up to the historical challenge to make it even better for our children and theirs. We will be given, as every generation before us has been given, all the divine aid necessary to further the principles on which we were founded. Democracy is profoundly relevant to the evolution of humanity, and as such it carries the psychological momentum to create miracles in the strangest places.

"To some generations," President Franklin D. Roosevelt declared in 1936, "much is given. From some generations, much is expected. This generation has a rendezvous with destiny."

So does ours. And we are accompanied on that rendezvous by invisible companions who were there for our forefathers and will be there for our children. Today, if we open our eyes to see, we will see that they are here for us.

1

MYSTICAL POLITICS

O N December 17, 1998, Bill Clinton became the second President in the history of the United States to be impeached by the House of Representatives. Many people, of course, thought that the impeachment was a good idea, a punishment fitting the President's transgressions. Yet the majority of Americans had made it clear in numerous polls that they favored a censure of the President rather than impeachment. Most people watched in disbelief as the Congress of the United States—or at least the party in power—took the basic position that the will of the people should not decide the issue, or even influence it to too great a degree.

The attitudes of those who favored impeachment are well documented, as are the attitudes of those who vociferously defended the President. But there are millions of Americans who neither loudly chastened nor loudly defended him. They are citizens who do not routinely make their political opinions heard one way or the other. They do not participate vigorously in American democracy, and often they do not even vote.

Once the impeachment occurred, however, many people awoke suddenly as if from a nap, feeling strangely disconcerted. What the hell was going on here? We hadn't meant for the political process to get this far out of our hands. We were skeptical about politicians, to be sure, but never before had the system seemed to be teetering on the edge of complete absurdity. All of a sudden, people were willing to get back into the political swing of things, if that was what was necessary to restore some reasonableness to public life. But we looked around and didn't know what to do to get back into the political game. We had been out so long that we couldn't find the door back in.

Speaking of politics, a lot of people said, "There must be a better way." You hear it once, you hear it twice. Pretty soon it becomes a buzz.

POLITICS has become the active involvement of an increasingly smaller subset of the American people. Out of 163 democracies in the world, we reportedly rank among the lowest in democratic participation. Instead of a broad-based citizen involvement, politics has become more of a spectator sport—a separate activity in which only some among us participate. This is hardly the sign of a healthy democracy. People have disengaged from the democratic process for many reasons, not the least of which is that the average person seems to feel that his or her personal involvement doesn't really make much difference. And those who for that reason no longer vote—who to the casual observer might seem not to care, who feel that there is no point in trying because some powerful elite has it all sewn up—*are increasingly correct in their assessment.*

Cynics have a point, after all. One look at the evening news, and it's clear that politics has become more of a trivial pursuit than a noble pursuit; the will of the people seems not to be the driving force of American policy; the general welfare of the people is arguably not the primary motivation of most governmental behavior. But if the American people don't take our government back, re-engaging a process we have chosen to ignore for a while, then we have no right to complain about those who would take it over in our absence. Those who can see what's wrong with the process are the last ones who should be sitting it out.

Yet where does one start? Many of us haven't been involved in political action for the last ten or twenty years, or more. Most Americans are so stressed out just trying to survive. The economic tension that pervades most American households—quite contrary to all the official protestations that the economy today is so good—makes worrying about politics go way down on the list of most people's priorities. People have had it with the government. It's not that we're apathetic about our country, but merely that we're disgusted with politics today. It's obviously a corrupt and sullied process, and how can fresh flowers grow in dirty water?

Still, with President Clinton's impeachment, a lot of people have started to wonder....

Dissent is in the air.

THOMAS Jefferson wrote to James Madison in 1787, "I hold it, that a little rebellion, now and then, is a good thing, and as necessary in the political world as storms in the physical." Healthy rebellion is not a *negative* emotion, but rather a politically legitimate expression of justified dissatisfaction. Dissatisfied people are often dissatisfied for a reason, and where we have no taste for rebellion, we have no taste for freedom.

If we do not rebel in some way against conditions that arouse our anger, then often the anger turns inward, becoming depression or even physical illness. Failing to question the root of the anger, our standard response these days is to merely mask the pain. There is nothing serene or transcendent about doing this; it is essentially a slave mentality.

All anger stems from a sense of limited freedom—freedom to be, to say, to feel, to do. In the United States particularly, people

—

unconsciously rebel against restrictions on our freedom because
we are aware this is supposedly the land of the free. The most
significant limits on our freedom today, however, are mainly hidden from view: we don't always see the connection between the
master's behavior and our own lack of health care, between
the master's behavior and our own economic insecurity, between
the master's behavior and our child's inadequate schooling.
But the most serious limitation of all is how limited we have become in our capacity to change things. People don't even know
anymore how to vote the master out of office, because the master
is so good at posing as a servant. On some level we all know this,
which only makes us angrier.

What would love do now, if called in to help us? Would it
transform the anger? Yes. Would it lead to destructive behavior?
No. Would it lead to rebellion? Yes, in a way. It would lead to divine rebellion. To nonviolent revolution. To the complete transformation of how we live with ourselves and how we live with
each other. To a re-envisioning of the entire world.

This is the time, and this is the place. A new millennium. A
new America . . . or else, just more of the same.

THIRTY years ago, America experienced its last rebellious generation, and looking back to the noisiness of the sixties gives us
insight into our relative quietude today.

During that decade, people were politically engaged, taking to
the streets to express our deepest passions about this country and
its behavior. Yet America was more innocent in those days, despite the violence of the times. We actually thought our rebellion
might *accomplish* something then, which few people seem to believe today.

The rebellious generation of the 1960s was ultimately quieted.
Something happened then to take us off the streets and to keep

us off. That something was violent threat and collective trauma, perpetrated on one generation and bequeathed to each one since as a legacy of those times.

The baby boomers were young at that time, and the young respond to dreams and visions. Those who carried aloft the most eloquent visions of a possible America during the 1960s were literally shot and killed in front of the eyes of the young who so adored them. For my generation, carrying a brilliant dream of a noble collective future meant putting oneself in the line of fire. From President Kennedy, to his brother Bobby, to Dr. King, to the students at Kent State, the primary articulators of positive change, of dreams for our democracy in this stunning age, were permanently silenced—*and the bullets that shot them psychically struck us all.* Millions of us became in many ways like the son of Robert Kennedy, who having watched his father murdered on television, got stoned and never recovered.

The invisible order that shot our heroes did not keep shooting, but began providing goods and services as quickly as possible to distract a grieving generation from our psychic pain. They did not leave us out of their conception of what America should be; quite to the contrary, they used us as their fodder, luring us into their planned environment of endless material consumption. We have been relatively quiet about anything meaningful ever since. Our leaders assassinated, our ranks dispersed, our generation received loud instructions: go home now, scatter, go to your rooms, and enjoy yourselves with all the toys we sell you.

We received a loud, silent message from those assassinations, an unconscious imprint that has become what psychologists call a "sponsoring belief" for an entire generation: "You can do pretty much whatever you want within the private sector. You will still be free, of course—to buy the red one or buy the blue one. *But leave the public sector alone.*" And no one had to say what sentence comes next: "Or we might kill you, too."

And so we did what we were told to do, and taught our children to do the same. We poured our prodigious talents and indisputable genius into the private domain. We left the public sector, which is essentially the political sector, to those—*whoever* they were—who wanted it so much that they were willing to go to such lengths to get it.

And thus we became a class of rich slaves. Our fear that what had happened to our slain leaders might happen to us, our naïve and immature preoccupation with drugs, and ultimately our complete seduction by a consumer society conspired to turn us into the greatest fuel source for the status quo that America has ever seen. Given our previous, youthful repudiation of the downside of American materialism, the irony here is almost grotesque. We who sought to heal America once before have helped to run her into the ground.

We have countenanced the undermining of our political system; we have tolerated the widening gap between rich and poor in America to levels deemed unsustainable by serious economic indicators; we have sold the health and welfare of our children and our environment to the highest bidders. Like Esau in the Book of Genesis, we have sold our birthright for a mess of pottage. Even more important, perhaps, we're so stoned on our very way of life, so distanced from our own authentic human knowing, that we hardly seem to realize what a black hole these things are forming in our national soul.

With every generation since the sixties, Americans have become more cynical, weary of politics, and too tired to dissent. Some would point to our frantic productivity and say that we're clearly on top of the world. As producers and consumers, certainly we are as active as ever. But as citizens we are anemic, not so much energized as propped up by artificial highs. Behind all manner of false merriment lies a river of Prozac. We tell ourselves these are the best of times, but in many ways it could be argued that we are collectively depressed. The children of God are not shining our lights at anything close to full wattage.

The baby-boomer generation is like a logjam in the river of American history; as long as we're psychologically stuck, everyone behind us remains somewhat stuck as well. We were born to proclaim that a better world is possible, yet then we were warned that to do so is not a good idea. We were thus distracted from our spiritual mission. We are not separate but one, and we long, at the deepest level of our being, to gift each other with our internal abundance, not manipulate each other for mere external gain.

We disengaged from politics after the 1960s because of a blow to our essential selves, and in the absence of that engagement, power has been usurped by the interests of a relative few. This is a spiritual crisis first and a political crisis second. America's real problem is our fear to express ourselves. Fear to be who we were born to be, and fear to do what we most long to do. We do not break through that fear by further disengagement. We break through the fear by embracing love.

What we longed for before, and what we long for now, is to love each other. And that is what the heroes of the sixties were saying. Looking back at the speeches of Dr. King or Robert Kennedy, one is struck by both the genius and the tragedy of their lives. They did not just say, "Let a man love his wife, or parents love their children." They said, *"Let us honor all life."* That is what made them so dangerous to the status quo. For that they lived, and for that they died. They pointed to the next step in America's moral evolution—the expansion of our compassion—and that is a step that by definition repudiates oppression and injustice.

Those of us who were young when our heroes were murdered have finally begun to reach middle age. We sometimes ask ourselves, "What will I say to myself on my deathbed? Will I know that I did what I came to earth to do?" And the answers don't always please us. For millions of people today, the thought that we might die knowing in our hearts that we didn't really go for it is actually scarier than the thought that they might kill us if we do.

Secrets still lurk regarding the political assassinations of the 1960s and they continue to haunt our collective psyche. Yet we have processed much in the last thirty years. The baby-boomer generation, having reached middle age, is finally beginning to mature emotionally. We have grieved, and we have begun to heal. Younger generations now contribute their own unique genius to the maelstrom of American society. There is a window of opportunity now for Americans to reclaim lost ground.

There is new possibility in the air today, a miraculous awakening and a change in the way we live our lives. It is a spiritual renaissance with social and political implications. Restoration and hope appear all over, as a rising environmental, community, and spiritual consciousness resurrects the dreams of former times. Civic brotherhood is beginning, in many, many places, to replace the false gods of self-centeredness and greed. There is a yearning among us to make right the world.

Will this become a broad-scale social force for good or merely isolated cases of cultural sanity? An America intending to heal itself will unscramble the information from which we have been systematically distracted for years, atone for and grieve our national errors, and consciously restore the political process to its role as an enlightened tool. It will take a miracle to do this, but miracles are always at issue in any great movement of history. Was not the American Revolution a miracle? Was not Indian independence from Britain a miracle? Are not miracles what our hearts most long for now?

Out of the ashes rises the phoenix. According to historian Arthur Schlesinger, Americans turn their attention to politics every thirty years. It has been thirty years since the end of the sixties, many Americans have been taking a deep look within, and what we have seen there casts light on many issues outside ourselves. There is darkness without, but no darkness, limitation, illusion, or fear can stand before the force of uplifted consciousness. Perhaps we are set to embark on a new chapter in our evolution as a nation, rededicating ourselves to the transcendental nature of democracy, declaring en masse our intention to have it rise at last to the level of its true potential.

"We have in our hearts," said Martin Luther King, Jr., "a power more powerful than bullets." It is time for us to use that power now, to free our nation and to free ourselves. Mystical power is the greatest power, in politics and in life. It reveals to us that bodies die but ideas do not, as long as people's hearts embrace them. It is time to resurrect the ideas that truly make this nation great. Where the sixties became a decade of death, may the millennium proclaim new life.

I once said to a friend of mine, another author who writes on spiritual subjects, "We really should be addressing political issues."

"Yeah," he responded, "I think you're right."

Then a pause, an angst-ridden silence.

"But there's only one problem," he said. "I really *hate* politics."

It's a conundrum: we don't want anything to do with politics because it's such a dirty business, yet turning away from it altogether makes us feel like we're avoiding something that maybe we shouldn't be avoiding.

Many people would love to feel that politics can be a high-minded effort, but it's hard to see how, in today's political climate. Particularly when looked at from a spiritual perspective, political involvement seems tawdry and low. It's the last place any of us look to anymore for hope or inspiration.

"I just want spirituality in my life," a friend said to me recently. "None of that other stuff matters to me."

And yet, what *is* spirituality? Is it just another compartment in our lives, like relationships, career, money, or health? Or is it something all-inclusive—the soul's oxygen, the life-giving agent meant to grace and revitalize all of life? If spirituality is relevant to anything, then it is relevant to everything. How can we speak seriously of a God who cares what happens to you and me, but somehow would not have *us* care about what happens to each other?

So how do we make spirituality relevant to politics? Ten years ago, if I asked that question, I would receive answers such as these:

- From political types, that "Spirituality is *not* relevant to politics. Don't start with all that spiritual stuff. It has nothing to do with politics. Politics is about the *real* world."
- From spiritual types, that "Spirituality makes politics irrelevant. Think about more positive things. Politics is just a low-level, addictive power game. Forget it. Real change can't come from there."

As we have seen, the last generation of Americans to seek a blend of philosophical and political flowering came of age in the 1960s. It's popular in some circles today to say, "Face it—the sixties didn't work." But for millions of Americans whose souls were branded forever by the magic of that time, to say it didn't work is a rather obvious attempt to kill whatever remnants of its audacious spirit might still remain alive.

To blend love and politics is indeed audacious. Politics is a fear-based pursuit in America today, and *love is the only thing that fear fears.* Love is the ultimate political rebellion. During the 1960s, love and politics were uttered in the same breath and sung in the same song. "All You Need Is Love" was a song we sang at *political* rallies.

And then, of course, the music died. By the mid-seventies, the paths of love and politics diverged. They would no longer seem even distantly related. Many who stayed interested in politics would come to trivialize the consciousness movement, and many of those interested in consciousness would start to ignore politics. Both sides then tended to smugly, self-righteously dismiss the other as irrelevant, thinking that they and they alone knew what it takes to change the world.

The consciousness movement concerns itself with addressing the causal level of events. All things in the outer world are reflections, or effects, of consciousness; mere changes in external conditions are thus seen as temporary palliatives, at best, for the problems of the world. Enlightened laws can be passed, but then repealed. Only when the mind has itself transformed does the world achieve any permanent change. The search for higher consciousness is the effort to attain a level of mind from whence only peace can flow, and in the presence of which only peace can exist.

Those interested in traditional politics, on the other hand, are primarily focused on the world of effects. They argue that we cannot afford to just sit around meditating while so much human suffering goes unchecked. They use the means of the material world to solve the problems of the material world, and are apt to see the issues of enlightenment as airy-fairy when applied to politics.

Today, it is the remarriage of our philosophical and political passions that holds the key to our political renewal. It is not either/or, but *both*—both cause *and* effect, mind *and* body—that need addressing in order to create a positive, effective politics for the twenty-first century. It is the political process itself that lacks, and that is because neither our hearts nor our higher minds are currently particularly active there. We need to recreate politics now as a mystical pursuit, bringing our souls to bear on the effort to make the world a better place.

And that is what is happening now. Many political types are saying, "Maybe politics really does need some deeper roots, some way to get past all the hatred"; and spiritual types are saying, "We need to extend the principles of enlightenment into social and political realms."

From the early American Quakers to Henry David Thoreau, to Mahatma Gandhi, to Martin Luther King, Jr., the effort to bridge the inner-outer duality has been one of the high points of human philosophy and endeavor. America has been fertile ground for such philosophy since our earliest days. It is the message that our spiritual and political evolution are not separate, but intimately and potentially even gloriously connected. It's the suggestion that we can't give to the world what we have not achieved within ourselves, and we can't keep for ourselves what we have not yet given to the world. And ultimately, it's the message that maybe, just maybe, love will someday rule the world.

IN the most advanced stages of ancient Egyptian culture, the Pharaoh was not just given his job for life. At regular intervals, he had to prove to his people that he still had what it took to do the job, displaying physical, moral, and mental strengths for all his subjects to witness. Similarly, statues of ancient Egyptian gods were reconsecrated yearly through prayer and rituals, as though it could not be taken for granted that the genuine *force* behind material substance would remain fully active without a regular reassertion of human devotion.

So it is that while Americans still go through the rites of democracy—political campaigns, elections, inaugurations— there is among us the sinking feeling that these rites are losing their spiritual *force*. Anything, no matter how initially pure, becomes corrupted if it is no longer connected to people's hearts. And that is how so many of us feel today. Democracy, we know, is still a vital concept—in fact, more so now than ever. But American democracy today is like a beautiful treasure housed in a decrepit building; our democratic principles are too good for our politics.

The state of our politics reflects the state of our humanity. In order to renew our politics, we're going to have to take a good look at the principles, or lack of them, that underlie all of American society today. As long as our social order rests on obsolete principles—obsolete because they are spiritually blind—there will be no real breakthrough in our political realities. In the words of Gandhi, "The problem with humanity is that we are not in our right minds."

The principles underlying our social, political, and economic conditions deem us purely material rather than spiritual beings, economics rather than relationship-oriented, and separate bodies rather than united hearts. We view competition as the primary motivator of human creativity, which it certainly is not. We view the creation of wealth as the primary goal of human work, though it should not be. We treat each other as anything but brothers, though that is what we are. These misperceptions of who we are and why we are here are central to the problems of the world. They are illusions holding back the human race, keeping us limited to the lower energies of dense, material-plane consciousness at a time when we are ready to expand to new levels of awareness and joy. In withdrawing our attachment to them, in rejecting their claim on our imaginations, we can transform our experience of life on earth.

A philosophical shift of historical importance is occurring throughout the world. Yes, we know that we are rational beings. Yes, we know that the physical world is based on the laws of science. And we also know—or remember at last—that in fact we are spiritual beings.

We are each of us divine essence, placed on earth to create the good, the true, and the beautiful. That goal is a compelling force that motivates us to higher heights than any contest or economic stimulus could ever come close to matching. There are within each of us God-given talents that do not respond to market pressure, yet spring to life in the presence of honor and respect. The spirit within compels us to serve each other rather than compete with each other, bless each other rather than condemn each other, and place our primary attention on the extension of brotherly love.

The dawn of the twenty-first century is a crossroads for the human race. We are living at a time of both intensified fear and intensified love, both encroaching barbarism and spiritual renaissance. Our consciousness now is backed by so much material power that, whether it is attuned to fear or attuned to love affects the future of the entire human race.

The spiritual renaissance of our time is like a mystical revolution of human consciousness, a surge of energy from the subconscious of a species that registers threat yet is intent upon survival. Love, like fear, is contagious. Unlike fear, however, love has ultimate authority over the forces of the world. It proceeds in spite of all obstruction. Every day, like the inevitable dawn, more spiritual light seeps into the world.

Awareness of spiritual tenets already colors our philosophical outlook as we approach the new millennium—in time, it will dominate our politics and economics, too. Either love will begin to rule the world or we will suffer the consequences of our continued resistance to the supreme law of the Creator—*that we love one another*—too long past the point when as a species we knew better. To run counter to love is to run counter to life. One cannot do so forever and survive. That is true for a person and it is true for nation.

In the 1960s, these words were written by Dr. Martin Luther King, Jr.:

> We are witnessing in our day the birth of a new age, with a new structure of freedom and justice.
>
> Now, as we face the fact of this new, emerging world, we must face the responsibilities that come along with it. A new age brings with it new challenges. . . .
>
> First, we are challenged to rise above the narrow confines of our individualistic concerns to the broader concerns of all humanity. The new world is a world of geographical togetherness. This means that no individual or nation can live alone. We must all learn to live together, or we will be forced to die together.
>
> . . . Through our scientific genius we have made of the world a neighborhood; now through our moral and spiritual genius we must make of it brotherhood. We are all involved in the single process. Whatever affects one directly affects all indirectly. We are all links in the great chain of humanity. . . . We have before us the glorious opportunity to inject a new dimension of love into the veins of our civilization.

The love so many of us would like to see injected into the veins of civilization must first pour into us. Society will not transform until we transform; what's wrong "out there" is but a mere reflection of what's wrong "in here." This is liberating news if we see it that way. Once we recognize that our minds are the causal level of worldly events, then we are free to seek to change the world by changing our thoughts *about* the world.

Racial tension, decivilization of our cities, violence and drugs among our youth and in our neighborhoods, economic disparity between rich and poor, global strife, threats of terrorism at home and abroad—the most serious problems we face as a nation are not actually solvable through traditional political means because they are the wounds of an internal disease. To simply imprison more criminals is not going to stop crime; to raise interest rates more or less is not going to make the American economy both abundant and just; and no amount of military might can ultimately control the bonfire of ethnic hatred if it continues to erupt like wildfire all around the world.

Tax cuts do not transform lives, and mere treatment of symptoms is not an adequate response to the diseases that plague us. A new law here and a new law there are little more than different Band-Aids on a ripped-apart aorta. We need a nonviolent assumption of the power of the soul to heal the pain of a world that has forgotten it has one.

Internal forces are bubbling up today like volcanoes of spiritual light. The extraordinary technological changes on our horizon are mere adjuncts to the even greater explosion of possibilities within the human mind. It is not only the interconnectedness of our computers but also the interconnectedness of our minds and hearts, that offer new and miraculous opportunities to mend the broken pieces of the world.

The bridge to a better world is a shift in mass consciousness, to a part of ourselves we have tended to keep out of the public realm. That part of us is not interested in traditional politics. It is neither a bridge to the past nor a bridge to the future, but a bridge to who we most deeply are.

It is who we are when we are hushed in church, near tears when they blow the shofar on Yom Kippur, honest and vulnerable with our therapist. It is the part of us least acknowledged, maintained, or seemingly even valued at all by the social order we have created around us. It is the part of us that still hopes for miracles and at times can even see them.

That place in each of us is the place of our true power; it is the key to our personal and political salvation. For it is from that inner, sacred place that we genuinely join with others. From elsewhere in the personality we can forge alliances, but we cannot merge. And from joining we emerge truly changed, having fertilized the garden that could yet become our Eden. We turn our backs on our lower natures, allowing the angels to breathe within us.

In every area of human endeavor, we see the reflection of a basic spiritual and psychological principle: where people join, breakthroughs occur. Where we are separate from each other—angry, polarized, and defensive—breakdown and disorder are inevitable. The way to heal social disorder, domestically or internationally, is to find our spiritual oneness. We don't need deeper analysis of our sicknesses so much as we desperately need a more passionate embrace of the only thing that heals them all.

Within the next ten years, America will experience a rebirth or a catastrophe. We have lost our spiritual rudder, and without it we have neither individual nor collective wisdom. Our culture has lost its sense of sacred connection to any power or authority higher than ourselves. Our national conscience is barely alive as we slither like snakes across a desert floor toward any hole where money lies. Nothing short of an internal awakening will heal us. Our children are prey to violence more vicious than that of most civilized countries, thousands of our young are themselves violent criminals, consider the condition of our biosphere (scientists from around the world consider the condition of our biosphere dangerously compromised), and millions of Americans can barely contain their rage much longer in the face of continued social and economic injustice. We see both major political parties steering the discussion of what truly ails us away from that which actually does, for they have no context for a higher discussion. They are now more alike than different, and neither is any longer home to truly serious political alternatives. They have become a game unto themselves. Our political salvation will not come from our political system as it now exists. It will come from deep within us.

• • •

JUST as Dr. King spoke of the interconnectedness of all beings, we are also more conscious today of the interconnectedness of all *aspects* of our being. The brokenness of the outer world reflects the brokenness within ourselves.

The awareness of an internal oneness, often called holistic thinking, posits the unity of mind, body, and spirit. Mind and body are not separate, machinelike components of a compartmentalized self, although the thought that they are—the Newtonian paradigm—has permeated the present age. It has influenced our politics, our medicine, even our relationships to one another. But the world is now awakening from the false premises of a mechanistic worldview, representing one of the most profound revolutions in the history of human thought. In time, that awakening will be brought to bear on every aspect of our lives.

The mechanistic worldview, exalted in the Age of Enlightenment, was the philosophical outgrowth of Newtonian science. Sir Isaac Newton deemed the world to be like a great machine, which could be understood, and then mastered, through rational thought. At its time, the Newtonian scientific revolution represented a liberating advance in how human beings viewed their world, repudiating superstition and false mystification in favor of the exercise of reason. Several of our Founders—James Madison, Alexander Hamilton, and John Adams among them— aspired to be the Newton of politics and government, and the glories as well as the limitations of our American political system are rooted in their rationalistic sensibilities.

Now, at the end of the twentieth century, science has corrected and improved upon Newtonian physics. Heisenberg, Bohr, Einstein, and others established the principles of quantum physics, proving that reality is not quite as solid or objective or deterministic as Newton thought. As British physicist Sir James Jeans proclaimed, the world now turned out to be "not so much a great machine as a great thought." Some "unreasonable" things are now proved to be true: time flows at different rates for observers moving at different speeds, solid atoms are largely empty, subatomic phenomena are both particles and waves, particles seem to affect each other at a distance even in the absence of a known causal connection, and, according to Heisenberg's Uncertainty Principle, an object is affected by the act of being observed. Adding to the astounding conclusions of modern physicists, contemporary biologist Rupert Sheldrake has posited the notion of "morphic resonance," suggesting that there is a unified field of consciousness connecting all life.

Quantum physics gives human consciousness a much more central role in the larger scheme of the universe than did Newtonian science, and this influences our philosophic as well as our scientific outlook at the turn of the millennium. How we perceive and how we interpret things are clearly more than mere symbolic powers, opening the modern mind to a more spiritual interpretation of reality than has been intellectually in vogue for centuries. "The more I study physics," said Einstein, "the more I am drawn to metaphysics." Ironically, it is science that both cast out the soul and then brought it back, into the consciousness of modern man.

Our Founders were revolutionary and, for their time, modern thinkers, applying the then cutting-edge science and philosophy of Newton to the politics of their age. Should we not apply, in our time, the principles of modern physics and philosophy to the politics of our own? John Adams ascribed to be this nation's political Isaac Newton; perhaps someone needs to come along and become our political Rupert Sheldrake.

In the words of Thomas Jefferson:

> I am not an advocate for frequent changes in laws and constitutions, but laws and institutions must go hand in hand with the progress of the human mind. As that becomes more developed, more enlightened, as new discoveries are made, new truths discovered and manners and opinions change, with the change of circumstances, institutions must advance also to keep pace with the times. We might as well require a man to wear still the coat which fitted him when a boy as civilized society to remain ever under the regimen of their barbarous ancestors.

Today, the rationalism of the European Enlightenment is being repudiated by a more soulful worldview, just as in a previous age, Renaissance and Enlightenment philosophy repudiated the overly mystified thinking of the Middle Ages. In every historical era there ensues a creative argument with the past, moving humanity either backwards or forwards depending on who's in charge. The progress of thought determines the course of human history, and our understanding of both the Newtonian hold on the era now passing and the quantum possibilities of the age now upon us, provide the tools we need to create a more enlightened future.

TRANSCENDENT democratic forces have always been in the American air, with deep and penetrating roots in our history. The Quakers of early Pennsylvania, for example, fostered many of the enlightened attitudes inherent in the U.S. Constitution toward religion, freedom, and the rights of the individual.

Pennsylvania Quakers held profoundly inward-turning spiritual beliefs. They had no ministers, but rather believed in "a universal priesthood of all believers." They believed God's spirit is alive in every human being, this spirit to be accessed not through the written word but through the exercise of conscience. In order to live a life of true religious purity, they claimed, we are to constantly look inward to what they called the "Inner Light."

This mystical philosophy was the guiding influence on Pennsylvania Quakers during the earliest days of this country; as such, it is as traditionally American as anything can possibly be. Quaker influence continued and spread. During the 1800s, Transcendentalism became a major philosophical movement in the United States. Inspired by the Quaker notion of an internal source of light, its main thrust was the exaltation of the role of intuition in connecting the individual to ultimate truth. American writers such as Ralph Waldo Emerson, Henry David Thoreau, and Walt Whitman created the glory and poetry of the Transcendentalist movement. They formed a counterforce to the materialistic worldview of the approaching industrial era, seeking in whatever way they could to preserve the power of the American soul in the face of a technological onslaught.

In addition to the role of intuition, and in keeping with the Quaker emphasis on conscience, Thoreau, in his essay called "Civil Disobedience," put forth the historic proposition that following the dictates of one's conscience is more important than following the dictates of one's government. That groundbreaking assertion became the basis for many subsequent political developments, including the prosecution of Nazi war criminals during the Nuremberg Trials following World War II.

In India in 1929, Mahatma Gandhi wrote in a letter to a friend that Thoreau's essay had "deeply impressed" him. Inspired in part by the message he garnered there, Gandhi founded the Indian Independence Movement, organizing a massive resistance to the British colonial occupation of India. He developed an entire political philosophy—calling it the philosophy of nonviolence—to harness the "soulpower" of the Indian people as an instrument of their common good.

Gandhi, himself a Hindu, believed in a universal spiritual Truth reflected in all the great religious teachings of the world. He wasn't seeking to use spiritual power to achieve a political end; rather, he exalted a state of spirituality from which political healing naturally results. Today's spiritual renaissance echoes that idea. As it is written in *A Course in Miracles,* "All expressions of love are maximal. . . . Miracles occur naturally as expressions of love." Political healing flows from spiritual experience because *all* healing flows from spiritual experience.

According to Gandhi, a nation has a soul just as an individual has one, and living for others is the key to the deliverance of both. An early holistic thinker, Gandhi claimed that if a nation's soul is healthy, its politics will be healthy. He promulgated the idea (*sarvodaya*) that spiritual power can socialize human relationships and be used as a political force. He claimed that spirit both works through matter and makes it harmonious; that it leads to the total blossoming of the individual, physically, mentally, and spiritually; and that the force of spiritual truth is greater than any army, weapons of destruction, or political authority (*satyagraha*).

From the viewpoint of nonviolence, the political realm is sacred. That is not to say that it becomes religionized; it is infused not with dogma but with faith in the power of love to heal and sustain all things. In the words of Gandhi, "Is not politics a part of the *dharma* too?"

Gandhi wrote:

Non-violence is the law of our species as violence is the law of the brute. The spirit lies dormant in the brute and it knows no law but that of physical might. The dignity of man requires obedience to a higher law, to the strength of the spirit.

Non-violence is a power which can be wielded equally by all children, young men and women or grown-up people, provided they have a living faith in the God of Love and have therefore equal Love for all mankind. When non-violence is accepted as the law of life, it must pervade the whole being and not be applied to isolated acts.

The very first step in non-violence is that we cultivate in our daily life, as between ourselves, truthfulness, humility, tolerance, loving kindness.

Non-violence is an unchangeable creed. It has to be pursued in the face of violence raging around you. The path of true non-violence requires much more courage than violence.

The restoration of India's independence was secondary to Gandhi; what he wanted was the restoration of India's soul. Gandhi, and later Martin Luther King, Jr., sought first to address the battered spirits of their people and then to treat the external wounds that the battering produced. They recognized that all political problems were rooted in spiritual wounds.

Just as Gandhi had been influenced by Thoreau, Martin Luther King, Jr., would then be influenced by Gandhi. Finding great inspiration in Gandhi's teachings, Dr. King traveled to India and then enthusiastically applied the principles of nonviolence to the crusade for civil rights in America. According to both, nonviolence is the love of God alive in every human heart, permeating every aspect of life, whether immaterial or material. There is no wound it cannot heal.

Dr. King said of Gandhi, "He was probably the first person in history to lift the love ethic of Jesus above mere interaction between individuals to a powerful effective social force on a large scale." Gandhi asserted the notion—and both men displayed it— that "soul force is more powerful than brute force." He claimed that nonviolence carries more power than any military army, weapon of destruction, or political authority; what we lack is belief that this is so. It is mental and spiritual weakness, more than external weakness, which holds us back. Having been trained to focus our eyes outward, most of us are apt to lack faith in the internal powers. Yet, while invisible to the physical eye, nonviolence awaits our decision to use it as a social and political tool. It is the endless and all-powerful love of God, active in the affairs of humanity *when it is channeled through us for that purpose.*

What Gandhi saw in British colonialism, and Dr. King saw in American institutionalized racism, were superior worldly powers. Yet they knew that because those were powers of might *but not right,* they would bow in time before the power of God's love. "The arc of the moral universe is long," said Dr. King, "but it bends toward justice." The nonviolent political movements working for independence in India and civil rights in the United States called for the power of love to triumph over the forces of hate.

A cornerstone of nonviolent philosophy is the notion that violence cannot defeat violence. The opponent is not someone we seek to defeat, but someone whose conscience we seek to arouse. Our conscience is never aroused by someone who hates us, but only by someone who honors us.

In his book *Stride Toward Freedom: The Montgomery Story,* Dr. King wrote the following about nonviolence:

> Non-violence in the truest sense is not a strategy that one uses simply because it is expedient at the moment; non-violence is ultimately a way of life that men live by because of the sheer morality of its claim. . . .
> It is not a method of stagnant passivity. The phrase "passive

resistance" often gives the false impression that this is a do-nothing method in which the resister quietly and passively accepts evil. But nothing is further from the truth. For while the non-violent resister is passive in the sense that he is not physically aggressive toward his opponent, his mind and emotions are always active, constantly seeking to persuade his opponent that he is wrong. The method is passive physically but strongly active spiritually. It is not passive non-resistance to evil, it is active non-violent resistance to evil.

Our dedication, then, is not just to a political goal but to a new way of life. While the desegregation of the American South was the political goal of the civil rights community, Dr. King said that its ultimate goal was a redeemed world. More than mere political change would be necessary to bring that about. "Our goal is to create a beloved community," he said, "and this will require a qualitative change in our souls as well as a quantitative change in our lives."

That, of course, is the hard part. For both Gandhi and King, the "coherence of ends and means" is a first principle of nonviolent philosophy. This means that who we are is as important as what we do, that how we go about change determines what ultimately *will* be changed, and the process itself is as important as the goal. The end, therefore, does not justify the means because, in fact, the goal is *inherent* in the means. In the words of Dr. King, "The means must be as pure as the end, for in the long run of history, immoral destructive means cannot bring about moral and constructive ends."

Transforming our own hearts is thus a prerequisite for transforming the world. *We will not achieve any higher-minded political goals until we transform the political process, and we cannot transform the political process without transforming ourselves.* We need less to get the message out than to get the message *in.* As Gandhi said, "My life is my message."

Thus, personal transformation becomes a social and political issue if we are interested in the development of a "holistic politics." If we've been spending several years asking, "Who am I?", the next question becomes "What should I do?" If we've been focused on the question, "What should I do?," we now start asking, "Who am I?" Those two questions actually *answer each other;* their being asked together creates the force we need in the world today. In the words of Neale Donald Walsch, author of *Conversations with God,* "Every act is an act of self-definition." Our acts define our being, and our being determines the ultimate power of our acts.

IT is the transcendent power of God within us that will "doeth the work" of healing the world, if we will devote ourselves to the emergence of that power. In order to express Him, first we must find Him. Gandhi said that the leader of the Indian independence movement was not him, but "the small still voice within."

According to Dr. King, the steps of nonviolence demand that "self-purification precedes direct political action." We can't be instruments of peace if we ourselves are full of emotional violence. The difficulty this poses for spiritual seekers is that to be interested in politics at all today is to be tempted to indulge our rage.

Watching President Clinton's impeachment trial on television, I noticed that the more I saw, the more judgmental I became toward those who obviously didn't agree with my views of the situation. But slowly my focus began to shift, to transfer from those on the screen to myself.

"Where's all that *love* inside you, Ms. Spiritual/Politics?" I asked myself. Where was my love, indeed, and what was its relationship to the angry, self-righteous woman railing against the President's accusers? So much for my dedication to nonviolence. I turned off the TV and began to pray.

I drifted into a gentle meditation where, much to my surprise, I found myself washing Bob Barr's feet! I saw angels ministering to Trent Lott! I found myself praying for Tom DeLay's peace and happiness. I knew that I must be onto something, because those thoughts clearly did not come from my day-to-day, conscious mind. They came from a thought system beyond my own. They came, in fact, from the sea of nonviolence, the eternal source of love and power that holds the key to our political as well as our personal salvation. "First heal yourself, Ms. Williamson. Then we'll think about addressing the rest of the world."

Dr. King often said how grateful he was that God didn't say we have to *like* our enemies! What we are seeking here is not a "personal love," but an "impersonal love." King was inspired by the notion in ancient Greek philosophy of the varieties of love: *eros, philia,* and *agape. Eros* is romantic love, which obviously won't save the world. Even *philia,* or love among friends, lacks the spiritual power to block the world's decline; it is easy enough to love people who agree with us. Rather, it is *agape*—our capacity to love even those whom we do not like—that has the power to restore the world to its innocence and grace.

MARTIN Luther King, Jr., said we need "tough minds and tender hearts." Many tough-minded thinkers in America today seem to lack heart, yet many of the most tender-hearted among us need to read a book or two! It's in the blend of the tough and the tender, the mystical marriage of our minds and our hearts, that we find the key to both our personal and our political healing.

The most important thing for us to consider today is how to harmonize our internal and external changes. When I met the Dalai Lama in India in 1996, I asked him, "Your Holiness, if enough of us meditate, will that save the world?" He leaned toward me and said, "I would answer you in reverse. If we want to save the world, we must have a plan. But no plan will work unless we meditate." I then asked His Holiness another question, to which he responded in a powerful way. I asked him how to apply his philosophy to the state of American politics. "That," he said pointedly, "is something Americans need to figure out."

Indeed, we must. Soul without body is ineffective in the world, and body without soul is dangerous. They are yin and yang; they need each other. An emphasis on "being" precedes all-powerful "doing." Put together in the service of a higher good, they create an enlightened politics—an aspect of the most compassionate life.

2

DREAMS AND PRINCIPLES

M o s t all Americans were raised to believe, and continue to be inspired by the thought, that America is a place where dreams come true. People came to this country, and continue to come—from villages and cities, farmlands and mountains, every continent and religious orientation—in search of a better life. They have traveled, often against unimaginable odds, packed like sardines in ships and boxcars, with an almost superhuman perseverance. They have desperately climbed walls while soldiers shot at their backs. They have rushed, clutching babies, to cross superhighways without getting run over, knowing that even if they made it across, border guards awaited them on the other side. Whether they came two hundred years ago or two months ago, escaping religious persecution or crushing poverty, their hearts were hearkening to the same song of hope: "Get to the United States. In the United States, things might be better."

Unless your ancestors were slaves brought here from Africa, then someone came to this country in hopes of finding an easier life. Someone's prayer—regardless of whom your ancestors were—was that you might someday have a better life than his or hers, that you might live the American Dream.

A most pertinent question at this time in our history is, "What is the American Dream?" How we answer that question goes far toward defining our relationship to citizenship and to democracy itself. Sometimes we cynically dismiss the idea of an American Dream, spitting at the suffering of millions to whom the concept meant everything, absolutely everything. Surely it behooves us to ask, "What is this thing for which so many have lived and died? What is this gift that I have been given, yet which I often treat as though it is no gift at all?"

We are used to politicians exploiting the concept of the American Dream, using the phrase casually as though all of us understand what it means. But in fact it can mean several things, and in the last few decades, we have clearly emphasized its material rather than its philosophical implications. Is the American Dream a social and political concept—that everyone here can be free? Or is it an economic concept—that anyone here can get rich?

At the end of the twentieth century, the American Dream is defined by most public leaders in primarily economic terms. Economic progress is deemed synonymous with social progress—if the economy is booming, then America must be doing great! But such an assumption bears a closer look. There are, in fact, powerful countries in the world today—China, for instance—that have adopted economic freedoms while suppressing social and political ones. Money—either the fun of having it or the stress of achieving it—can easily distract us from essential truths regarding the nature of freedom itself.

If our bottom line is money, then we have committed to materialistic values. But if our bottom line is the dream of freedom, then the most important things are not material, and many things are more important than money. Money, like tears, can easily blur our vision. It can seem that because we have money, the dream is alive and well by definition. Or because we don't have money, we don't have a lot of time to think about it one way or the other. Or while it's true we don't have much money ourselves, we keep hearing constantly how good the economy is doing, so the dream must be flourishing for *someone*!

In fact, there is much more to freedom than economics. If our dream is merely to make money, then we're dreaming small—we're not asking for too much but for too little. We were born, as Americans, into the philosophical promise that here, in these United States, humanity could make its dreams come true. And the highest state of dreaming, for a person or for a nation, is not that we will *get* something, but that we will *become* someone. From that state of being flows all abundance. Alan Greenspan doesn't control the flow; consciousness controls the flow.

What our souls truly long for is a state of being, and contrary to the insidious lies of advertising, that state cannot be bought. Money cannot buy internal freedom. It can in many cases buy the things we *think* will make us feel free, but like Dorothy when she finally meets the Wizard of Oz, we will always at last be forced to see that *things* have no power to take us home. Home is what we long for, but home is not a material but a spiritual condition. We will not be home until we truly, deeply love one another. When that occurs, money will not be allowed to interfere with the commitment. Healthy competition, yes; exploitation and domination, no. And from our spiritually rising up that way, we will counterintuitively learn the true secret of material abundance: that it flows more effectively from love than from fear. Spiritual wisdom will be the key to wealth in the twenty-first century. Thinking that we *need* the material world makes us slaves to the material world; knowing that we are not *of* the material world turns us into its masters.

The fact that the American Dream has historically been driven, not by money, but by dedication to the creation and maintenance of liberty is the spiritual blessing that has *drawn* to us such extraordinary material fortune. As we have sought to bless humanity, so God has clearly blessed us. Our dollar bill is inscribed with a mystical seal bearing the symbol of brotherly love. Nothing threatens our social order—including our economics—more than a diminished commitment to the dream proclaimed on that seal.

We are currently living at a time when the needs of the marketplace are placed so high above the needs of people, here and around the world, that hardly anyone feels free anymore to question the values implied by that shift. But question it we'd better, if we're interested in bequeathing democracy to our children as others, at often such great cost, had the courage to bequeath it to us.

As a nation, we have a collective psyche, a common river of thoughts and feelings that runs through the soul of every American. That river runs beneath our dreaming like an underground source of nourishment and aid—America's emotional Nile.

The American Dream, when best understood, is the fact that we have the right to dream at all. It is the right to expect that our talents and abilities and diligence—not the prejudices of others—will determine the nature of the lives we live. That is a spiritual principle and a radical thought to which the nation was committed at its founding. While reality often contradicts the dream, and various forces would seek to squelch it, the American Dream stays alive within the collective mind.

A national dream, in order to remain viable, must be as a spark reignited in the heart of each generation. Otherwise, our river of hope dries up. A dream doesn't rest on reason but, rather, flies on the wings of passion, and unfortunately, most modern education systems do not honor passion. We are not taught to love our great historical truths but merely perhaps to memorize them. For far too many of us, the embrace of essential democratic principles has not been the re-enactment of a courageous, experiential response to the darkness of ancestral history, but merely a mechanical recitation of words. And yet poignantly, many millions of Americans would still willingly risk their lives for these principles. There is something in us well aware of an inutterably precious nugget of truth in the vision of our forefathers, which in some mysterious way still applies to each of us.

Our right to dream whatever life we wish for ourselves, and our responsibility to respect the dreams of others, is the fulcrum of the American ideal. Even in the most oppressive societies, *some* people have the right to dream. What makes a free society different is that we are *all* supposed to have that right, and a reasonable opportunity to make our dreams come true.

Many people in America have lived lives of very limited, even cruelly squelched dreams, not through any fault of their own but through accidents of history and various forms of obstruction and injustice. That has been true in the past and it is true today. To deny this is not to honor the dream but to mock it. If any Americans are denied the right to weave their dreams, then America itself isn't weaving hers. It is the job of every generation of Americans to further expand and fulfill the dream of freedom and justice for all.

In former generations, both bondage and freedom had mainly a material face. Slavery, oppression, and injustice were externalized, therefore our dreams of ending them were made external as well. In ending slavery, we committed to the dream. In passing child labor laws, we committed to the dream. In passing civil rights legislation, we committed to the dream. Every generation plays out the struggle between those that would expand the dream and those that would constrict it. Reinterpreting the American Dream to mean very little more than a job that pays well is to rob it of its deeper meaning. Now, in order to expand the dream of freedom for the times in which we live, our main responsibility is to re-examine the meaning of both freedom and bondage.

Today, our states of bondage are not material so much as emotional and psychological and spiritual, and all states of material bondage still existing would disappear in a moment were we to free our hearts and minds. What we most need to be free of now is our tendency to distract ourselves from the pain of the world, our tendency to isolate rather than join with others, our own selfishness and narcissism and unforgiveness and greed. Those tendencies are not our sins, but our wounds. They are our modern prisons, and the modern version of the American Dream is to break free of these chains within ourselves.

THE American Dream began with those who came here to escape their nightmares. Some, in fact, found their nightmares here. Our Founders were the oddest mix of all: they both articulated the dream for themselves and their children and, in the case of those who owned slaves, perpetrated a nightmare on others. Now we find ourselves, as their descendants, with the job of maintaining and extending our national dreams, and awakening from the horrors of our national nightmares.

Our Founders were not perfect people—a fact to be neither whitewashed nor ignored—but they reached nonetheless for extraordinary ideals and encased them in a Constitution that institutionalizes our liberty. They risked their lives, signing the Declaration of Independence, to make a historic break from the past—a past they deemed an unworthy template for the human experience. They changed the course of human events, reaching beyond the accepted boundaries of what was to be expected from life, stretching the limits of human possibility. They left in their wake a compelling promise, not only to Americans but also to people throughout the world, that a society could exist in which the individual talents and abilities of free, self-governed people could come together fruitfully, harnessed in the service of a collective good.

The founding of America is not a tale drawn from one-dimensional lives. Jefferson, Washington, Franklin, Madison, Hamilton, Adams, and Paine were very real people—nothing in their day like the formal and official portraits of them that now hang in polite museums. The same is true of their successors—the great American statesmen, political thinkers, social reformers, philosophers, writers, and artists who have helped us refound ourselves from that day to our own time.

In making wooden characters of very juicy people we have diminished our own connection to them. Jefferson almost did not emerge from his grief over the death of his wife, and years later wrote love letters to Maria Cosway that make *The Bridges of Madison County* look tame. Lincoln would bury his head in his hands each time news reports reached him of massive casualties in the Civil War, sobbing, "I cannot bear it, I cannot bear it." Polio victim Franklin D. Roosevelt clung to the arm of his son in a heroic effort to appear to walk on his own to the podium at the 1932 Democratic Convention, knowing that if Americans thought he could not walk that they would never elect him. He succeeded, and was then described by a friend as having been "cleansed, illumined and transformed by his pain."

What is important is not merely that we record history, or that we understand it from a seemingly objective perspective. What matters is that we take it personally, that we own it in the deepest part of ourselves, that we might solidify its power where it is something to be proud of and try to transform it where it is not.

The great figures of American history still reach us from the grave, having said and done things that affect each of us in a practical manner, every day of our lives. Their stories illuminate not only what happened before but most significantly what is

likely to happen again. We are challenged by an adequate knowledge of history to measure our lives in relation to it, to succeed
where others have faltered, to run the race that others ran, to try
to keep the wheels of history moving in a positive direction. The
past teaches us, most important, that the *movement of history in a
positive direction can never, ever be taken for granted.*

Yet we do take it for granted that we are the heirs of our
Founders' vision. Vigilance doesn't seem to be necessary now;
surely *someone* is watching the store. But there is no one here but
us, and more and more we might ask ourselves if we have not become, in our generation, more like the royalists who did not support the revolutionaries, who chose to remain in the yoke of
serfdom, trading the sometimes uncomfortable quest for freedom
for the comfort of false security. Our Founders asserted the dramatic proposition that if ordinary people are deliberative and responsible, then they can run the affairs of their nation. But today
we are not doing that. With our voter participation among the
lowest of any democracy in the world, we have allowed an un-
holy alliance of government—like a new monarchy—and corporate influence—like a new aristocracy—to take control of events
in a way that would have made our Founders shudder. Surely,
were they here now they would worry for the dream of liberty
that they weaved for their posterity. We have not lost our rights,
but neither are these rights profoundly secure. We are much like
a massively bleeding person who has not died *yet.* That person
will die unless transfused. And we will lose the precious blood of
our democratic freedoms if we do not wake up and we do not act.

We have become a distracted nation. We know more about the
lives of television actors than of our great historical figures, and
more about the way our toys work than the way our democracy
works. Yet there is a hunger rising among us to get back to the
things we forgot along the way.

The principles that our Founders elucidated in the Declaration of Independence, our Constitution, and our Bill of Rights, then continuing with Lincoln's Gettysburg Address, are the sacred powers at the core of American democracy. They are not rules but values. They act as pillars upholding the dynamic energy of American democracy, and they can handle any assault except the people's diminished commitment to them. It is seriously detrimental to our individual and collective good that the average American citizen can't quite tell you what those principles are.

Our democratic principles are the essential ingredients in the American Dream. They protect the dream and stave off the nightmares. They are the light at the center of our democratic hopes.

First Principles

America's first principles are simple and basic. They are undergirded by an even more basic idea: that we are a democracy and thus govern ourselves. These principles are guideposts for the process of doing so. They are the keys to our freedom and the freedom of our children.

Yet too few of us are passionate about these principles anymore. Citizenship means more than voting, paying taxes, or obeying laws. It is, when we choose it to be, a powerful expression of self, the absence of which makes it easy to steal from us the powers we have been granted.

America's first principles are not partisan issues. They are the things on which we have agreed to agree. We agree that all people should be equal before the law. We agree that power in America shall stem not from the government into the people but rather from the people into the government. We agree to seek to balance individual rights with protection of the general welfare.

—

And we agree that people shall have the right to freely practice and share their religious, social, and political beliefs without threat of external tyranny.

A nation "so conceived," in the words of Lincoln, is divinely inspired by the universal blessing inherent in these first principles. Divine inspiration is not a metaphor. From a spiritual perspective, it is a literal power to transcend and subsume all lesser ideas.

There are dramatic examples throughout our history of contests between those who would commit the nation to its stated principles and those who would compromise those principles for short-term personal or economic gain. The Civil War, for instance, pitted those who chose to hold the nation to its principle of equality for all against those who tried to secede from the Union rather than give up slavery and comply.

In other words, our governmental principles are often more advanced than we are, owing to the extraordinary prescience and genius of our Founders. In 1801, the newly elected President Jefferson admonished the nation to make "periodic recourse to first principles," relying on their power and the power of our collective agreement to adhere to them, to guide us as beacons through darkened times.

It is extremely rare that an issue comes up in American society that does not have light cast upon it by our first principles. They form America's political bedrock. Today, our problem is that most Americans do not know what those principles are. We were either taught them at school (where, for the most part, they're not even taught anymore!) and have forgotten them, or we actually never learned. We therefore tend to think of political negotiation as a fight between competing opinions, rather than a process by which we all work toward a higher realization of principles on which we already agree.

Our first principles stand outside of time, providing a stillness that keeps our nation centered through the centrifugal tides of historical change. Referring back to them collectively is an exercise of profound democratic authority. We have allowed the stresses and merchandising of modern life to lure our attention toward lesser things, creating a crisis in American democracy.

The first principles are our tools; every citizen needs to have them in his or her mental pocket. You don't have to be a lawyer to understand them; James Madison was the leading spirit among those who wrote the Constitution, and he was not a lawyer. You don't have to be a college graduate; George Washington was not a college graduate. You don't have to be a so-called expert to have a valid opinion. You don't have to be anything but a citizen, to be the source of power in the United States. In fact, that's the entire point of our power: that it belongs to "We, the People."

These principles are planted firmly in the soil of human conscience, and they are important for their spiritual as well as political significance. They hold power not only for us but also for people throughout the world, because they reflect the tenets of a *higher* law. Hearts around the world have hearkened to these principles, from French Revolutionaries in the eighteenth century to Chinese dissidents in Tiananmen Square.

And yet, for this country, only one thing matters: do *our* hearts hearken to them, now?

I once said to my then six-year-old daughter, an avid Barbie fan, "Darling, Barbie looks anorexic. Someone with a body like that would be in the hospital with a very bad disease. Her hair is stupid and her values are questionable. Do you think she ever does any charity work?" My daughter looked me squarely in the eye and said, "Mommy, I love who I love. I'm not going to change my thoughts." I gulped. I didn't agree with my child's opinion, but I was glad she was so quick to defend her right to have one. You're never too young to learn that you have the right to your opinions, and to your freedom to express them.

—

And you're never too old to make sure that no one ever, ever gets away with compromising that freedom, as long as you're around.

PRINCIPLE 1: EQUALITY OF RIGHTS AND OPPORTU-NITY: *That all of us are equal before God and should be treated that way by the American government.*

The higher point of our equality as Americans is not just that it reflects our Founders' thoughts but that it also reflects God's thoughts. To commit to equality is to submit to the will of God, that we should love each other as He loves us.

The wording of the Declaration of Independence is as follows: "We hold these truths to be self-evident, that all men are created equal, that they are endowed by their Creator with certain inalienable Rights, that among these are Life, Liberty and the pursuit of Happiness—That to secure these rights, Governments are instituted among Men, deriving their just powers from the consent of the governed."

This principle is easy to take for granted, until we remember exactly what it means. It means that in this country, it is not the circumstances of our birth, but the fact that we are American, that determines our rights and opportunities to pursue happiness. Note that the Declaration says it is the responsibility of government to *secure* those rights.

James Madison, the father of our Constitution, wrote, "Who are to be the electors of the federal representatives?" His response defined the ideal meaning of equality in America: "Not the rich more than the poor; not the learned more than the ignorant; not the haughty heirs of distinguished names more than the humble sons of obscure and unpropitious fortune."

The ideal of equality, and our progress toward its full manifestation, is central to American democracy. Regarding both rights and opportunities, equality as a first principle is seriously threatened in America today—yet the threat is largely underestimated. It is couched in words that imply we take equality for granted here, that *of course* we all believe in it, and therefore *we need not be vigilant on its behalf.*

Routinely today, however, this first principle is made to stand second or third in line. Yes, we have made strides—in civil rights, women's rights, and so on—but no, this is not the time to relax. Those with money today have become, in reality though not in principle, more "equal" than anyone else.

Corporate welfare (tax subsidies to our wealthiest corporations) increases to the tune of billions of dollars, while Head Start programs to the tune of millions are obliterated or turned over to already overburdened private charities. The American public is being asked to acquiesce in an unethical arrangement whereby we withdraw support from poor children to make sure that the children of parents more well off are taken care of in an even more privileged fashion. If we believe in the principle of equality, then the rich should not be granted greater opportunity than the poor.

Every time we take support away from nutritional, medical, educational, or job training and creation programs that benefit those who need them most—then give tax breaks or corporate subsidies to the far more privileged—we are attacking the first principle of equality in America. And that is the basic trend in American government today.

The most dramatic form of inequality in America now is economic inequality. The gap between rich and poor has been steadily increasing in this country for more than twenty years. In the words of the late Supreme Court Justice Louis Brandeis, "We can have a democratic society or we can have great concentrated wealth in the hands of a few. We cannot have both." Thomas Jefferson said that we must endlessly struggle for, and never be

—

complacent until we have achieved, equal opportunity for modest prosperity and equal treatment before the law of every American citizen. And economic inequality extends its unjust influence: criminal justice, for instance, is statistically biased in the United States. If you're poor in America today, your chances for justice are far less than if you're rich.

Where there is little adequate education—as in the inner cities of America—there is no equality of actual opportunity. Where there is little adequate health care—as among America's poor and even some of our middle class—there is no equality of actual opportunity. Where there are very few opportunities for true professional advancement—as is also true among America's poor—there is no equality of actual opportunity.

Many issues look different when seen through the lens of the first principle of equality—universal health care, education, and criminal justice, to name a few. The fear-based thinking of the world gives emphasis to our differences, and thus our separation. Such thinking diminishes our commitment to equality.

It's impossible to appreciate that our rights matter, without appreciating that our *personhood* matters. Every person matters; in that single thought lies the moral authority of American democracy. Our rights to free public education, free speech, a free press, and free association among ourselves—all of these freedoms exist to create and maintain our equality as citizens.

It is very important that we teach our children what this means, and why it matters. Our rights matter because *people* matter. No one is supposed to get to tell you what you can do or say in the United States, as long as it doesn't hurt anyone else. Anyone who understands history, or current world affairs, knows what an awesome blessing this is, and what gratitude we owe those who have given their lives to secure it, that we can assume in this country even minimum compliance to the principle of equality. Throughout the world, there are people living in fear that they might "disappear" if something they say or do offends the official order. Women in Afghanistan today, living under the Taliban regime, risk torture or death if they even *wear the wrong clothes*. The principle of equality is a very, very serious issue indeed.

Our equality before the law, theoretically, is not up for discussion. It is the birthright of every American; it is a *given*. But just because something is encoded in law doesn't mean we can take for granted its constant *enforcement*. The only way a legal principle remains safe is if it remains alive in our hearts. We must be ever vigilant that the law, and the principles which uphold it, are not compromised *while we're not looking*. To think otherwise is not "being positive," but childish.

Martin Luther King, Jr., used to say that he was not going to Washington to *ask* for rights for black Americans, but to demand the rights they had been given already. To threaten anyone's liberty is to threaten everyone's liberty. As my father used to say, "What they can do to anyone, they can one day do to you."

The political question, for instance, should not be, "What do you think of homosexuals?", but rather, "Do we or do we not remain commited to the principle of equality for all, and how does that principle apply to the quest for homosexual rights?" Whether someone in America *likes* someone else in America is irrelevent to what both of their rights should be before the law. The only way we can be vigilant on behalf of our children's freedom is if we are vigilant on behalf of *everyone's* freedom.

In the words of Martin Niemoller, a Lutheran pastor who was imprisoned by the Nazis for eight years because he spoke out against Hitler, "First, they came for the socialists, and I did not speak out because I was not a socialist. Then they came for the trade unionists, but I did not speak out because I was not a trade unionist. Then they came for the Jews, but I did not speak out because I was not a Jew. Then they came for me, and there was no one left to speak for me."

PRINCIPLE 2: E PLURIBUS UNUM: *That within our diversity lies a national unity—that we are at the same time a people who reflect and embody diversity, yet are united in our fealty to these treasured first principles.*

Our Founders were students, directly and indirectly, of a wide-ranging body of ideas and information. Both Benjamin Franklin and Thomas Jefferson were careful and respectful students, for instance, of the government and politics of the Iroquois Confederation and other Native American peoples.

In the Iroquois Indian Confederacy, different Native American tribes retained their individuality yet created a common network for the sake of progress and mutual protection. They were different, yet in certain ways they were one. Echoes of that governmental philosophy can be found in America's first principle called *E Pluribus Unum*, or "Unity in Diversity."

There are people in America who emphasize our unity yet fail to appreciate our diversity, just as there are those who emphasize our diversity yet fail to appreciate our unity. It is important to honor both. It is our unity *and* our diversity that matter, and their relationship to each other reflects a philosophical and political truth, which democracy requires.

Unity and diversity are not adversarial, but rather complementary elements in American society. Both make us better. We are woven from many diverse threads, yet we make one piece of fabric; we are many and one at once. You're Catholic *and* you're an American; you're gay *and* you're American; you're black *and* you're an American. Neither identity is to be sacrificed for the sake of the other.

When the country was founded, our diversity was determined mainly by our geographical dimension. Massachusetts was very different from the Carolinas; they remained true to their individual identities while at the same time forging one American culture. Our statehood now is a less critical geographical concept than an ideological one; our ethnicity, beliefs, and economics define our differing "states" today. We are different colors, different religions, different beliefs, and different cultures. Yet we are united in our fealty to these common principles. We are *all* Americans, and we are involved in a great experiment *together.* No group of Americans are the "normal" Americans, no group of Americans monopolize truth or wisdom or righteousness, and no group of Americans deserve more or less protection or opportunity from the American government.

It is when we have a healthy experience of our individual identity that we can most easily accept sharing a larger one. But that first step cannot be skipped; it's wrong to expect someone to play down his or her religious or racial identity in service to a larger identity until he or she has first been shown honor for what that individual identity is. I'll stop going on and on about being a woman once I feel you *respect* me as one. At that point— once we have all been acknowledged as individually significant —it's important that we turn our attention to the betterment and preservation of the nation we all share.

Unity in diversity is a principle demanding our personal maturity. We must develop the ability to tolerate the creative chaos of many voices and opinions all expressing themselves at once; to not seek control over the thoughts or behaviors of others just because they are different from us; and to listen with respect and recognize the dignity of those with whom we disagree. It is not a first principle in America that any one group gets to be *right.* It is a first principle that each of us, and each of the diverse cultures living together here, has valuable things to say and to contribute. Allowing everyone to do so is central to our liberty, our genius, and our progress toward a greater good.

As children of God, it's not just our equal rights that should be stressed but our equal brilliance as well. During the spring of 1998, I was invited to speak at a gathering hosted by the Gandhi Institute for Non-Violence, in Memphis, Tennessee. The event was called a Unity Banquet, held as part of the celebration of a Season for Non-Violence, in which eight different local ethnic groups shared some unique expression of their own cultures—dance, song, clothing, food, and so on. Young Muslim women did a magnificent performance piece, Mexican women modeled dresses from their native communities, small Chinese children gave a martial arts demonstration, Ukrainians shared ethnic foods, and the like. Before the event, I had no conscious prejudice against any of those groups. But neither had I the deeply profound respect and admiration for their cultures that I gained that day. I had never before been moved to tears by their unique contributions to the human spirit.

James Madison once said that "tolerance is not enough" because, psychologically, tolerance still implies judgment. In order to experience the highest possibilities of American culture, the social fruition of the ideal of *e pluribus unum*, we will need to do more than merely tolerate each other. America won't fulfill its most noble dream until we actually come to *admire* each other for the glorious characteristics of our uniquely individual ethnic identities. It is only when we have come to the point when we genuinely bless each other's children, and recognize their potential brilliance, that we will be on the path to the possible America.

There are many people in America today who "tolerate" others through clenched teeth, who "respectfully disagree" with a look that is chilling. Their look seems to say, "Until we take over, I accept that we haven't yet." America belongs to *all of us*. Equality means that none of us is inherently more valuable than anyone else. Freedom means that we actually like it that way.

PRINCIPLE 3: BALANCE OF INDIVIDUAL LIBERTY AND PROTECTION OF THE COMMON GOOD: *That it is the responsibility of government to protect the general welfare, yet with enough checks and balances to ensure that it remains limited enough to guarantee our individual liberties.*

America ideally seeks to balance the needs of the individual with the needs of the collective. This principle is central to our greatest achievements, but also to our greatest political battles.

Sometimes we're appalled because the government is getting into our business and we think it should keep its nose out; other times we're appalled because we feel the government hasn't adequately taken care of the collective good. When American politics is at its best, we create a healthy balance between the two.

Yes, it's true that we should protect the environment and the children, our most precious resources—but yes, it's also true that an individual should be free to pursue his or her own economic goals with as little interference or obstruction as possible. Yes, it's true that law enforcement officials should have the necessary power to protect us—but yes, it's also true that the individual should be protected from too much police or governmental interference. Collective welfare vs. individual rights; this is the dynamic tension underlying most political debate today, and it's amazing how passionate we get when we're revved up about one or the other.

"Don't you dare try to take away my right to own a gun" vs. "Can't the government get all these guns off the street?" "How dare the government try to tell me how to run my factory" vs. "Why can't the government protect the water in our lake from the chemicals in that factory?" What so often shows up as violent competition becomes, when we truly learn to *listen* to each other, the stuff of creative synergy. Freedom doesn't mean we will al-

ways agree; it means we all have important points of view to contribute to the mix.

President Eisenhower once said that the American mind at its
best is both conservative and liberal. We need to conserve those
things that are eternally true and still retain the ability to respond
liberally and spontaneously to the immediate demands of our
time. What's so lacking in American politics today are people
showing adequate respect for those who disagree with them. An
intelligent person can understand that both individual *and* collective rights are important to the nation. Depending on the issue,
liberals and conservatives stress different sides of the equation.

A true liberal doesn't think government can fix all our problems, and a true conservative doesn't believe that whatever is
good for General Motors is always good for America. Yet there
are many on both sides of our political debate who would stereo-
type their adversaries as thinking that way. What is lacking, obviously, is a civilized center. We have too little "golden mean" in
politics today. Somebody is always pointing a finger, it seems,
saying "He," "She," or "They" are the enemies of America. In
truth, the enemy of America is that pointed finger.

After the hardest-fought Presidential election of his time,
Thomas Jefferson reminded his countrymen, "We are all Republicans, we are all Federalists." Civic life in America *should* include
vigorous debate between liberals and conservatives; that is
democracy in action. But the debate must remain within the
bounds of mutual respect and dignity or our civil life is no
longer civil. Those who view political debate as merely "your
needs and desires vs. my needs and desires"—with no respect for
America's need to balance individual liberty with the common
good—bring down the political process.

Individual liberty matters *as well as* the collective good. I'm as
guilty as the next person of giving into anger when I feel
strongly about an issue and someone else either doesn't share my

passion or works to thwart the goals I feel are important. In the Preamble to the Constitution, it says, "We the people of the United States, in order to form a more perfect Union, establish justice, insure domestic tranquility, provide for the common defence, promote the general welfare, and secure the blessings of liberty to ourselves and our posterity, do ordain and establish this Constitution for the United States of America." To me, "promoting the general welfare" includes the care and protection of America's children.

I'm passionate about the fact that one-fifth of America's children live in poverty, that millions of our children go to schools in which there aren't even working toilets, in slums where the social and economic conditions are as dire as during the worst days of the Great Depression—while Congress fails to provide mass transit, adequate job-training programs, small-business loans, or greater nutritional and learning programs in those neighborhoods, while giving deeper and deeper tax cuts to the richest people among us. What I've learned, however, is that just because someone doesn't agree with me on this doesn't mean he or she is in some covert conspiracy with the Grinch who stole Christmas. Until I get that point at the deepest core of my being, I'm not part of a new politics. As long as I'm working against something I hate instead of *for* something I love, I'm of the old and not the new. The politics of a new America is a love for what could be and a reach for the possible.

It's hard at times to develop a nonviolent, loving, and respectful attitude toward those who do not agree with us. But anything less keeps us stuck on the political wheel of suffering. Saint Thomas Aquinas once wrote, "We must love them both, those whose opinions we share and those whose opinions we reject. For both have labored in the search for truth, and both have helped us in the finding of it." I'll write that out and put it on my bathroom mirror, if you'll write it out and put it on yours.

PRINCIPLE 4: RELIGIOUS FREEDOM: *That every American shall worship how he or she wishes, if he or she wishes, according to the individual's own conscience and with no governmental interference in that right.*

The separation of church and state was not meant to religiously constrict us, but rather to religiously free us. We were all taught as children that early Americans came to this country fleeing religious persecution, commited to the creation of a society in which no one could be told by the government either how to worship or even whether to worship. And neither would their new government be constricted in any way by an official religious dogma. Both government and religion are thereby protected from interference by the other. A thick line between church and state keeps our religious lives free of any government pressure and our government free of religious pressure. It is an enlightened and enlightening concept.

Our Founders did not seek to block the religious path but rather to free it of all obstruction. They recognized that religious dogma can be as detrimental to the human spirit as political dogma can be, and can often be used to restrict the rights of others. That was not to be allowed in the United States. Our founders themselves were men of spiritual conviction, though many of them would be hard pressed to meet the standard of what some fundamentalists call religious today. In the words of Thomas Jefferson, "I have sworn upon the altar of God eternal hostility against any form of tyranny over the mind of man." He recognized religious tyranny to be as oppressive as any other.

But separating the state from the undue influence of religious institutions was in no way meant by our Founders to be an impediment to the search for higher truth, within the individual or within society. They embraced the Creator while refusing to pay homage to specific dogmas claiming to monopolize religious

Truth. That stance was in support, not rejection, of the true religious experience. The separation of church and state was intended to *support* our spiritual flowering by guaranteeing its freedom.

Spirituality, to many of us, is as important to the soul as is oxygen to the body. Without it, the world can make sense to the mind but it can never make sense to the heart. But the spirit is an internal phenomenon, and civilization has always suffered when any particular dogma or doctrine has sought to impose itself upon the peoples of the world. The highest, most spirit-filled religious consciousness is a living water, and that water is poured into the world not through religious doctrine but through the human heart. Love itself is the highest religious experience. No religion has a monopoly on God because religion itself has no monopoly on God. God is looking to us for more than words alone; He is looking for our forgiveness, mercy, and love. Ecclesiastical, orthodox religious systems are not the only arbiters of spiritual force. They are not the only spiritual guides. We will not be renewed by a worldly religious authority, but by the spirit of God Himself.

Religious freedom, as an American first principle, means no one in America has a right to monopolize the religious discussion. Even today, people throughout the world face torture and murder for not seeing God the way someone else does. It is one of the cornerstones of American liberty that we make a stand for religious freedom. Jefferson wrote, "Toleration is not enough. What we need is liberty, fully protected by the law, to believe or not believe as you see fit." America was not founded to protect the definition of God as proposed by any one group or individual; it was founded to protect our liberty to think however we wish to think.

We must not indulge any group of Americans who seek to ban other people's conception of spirituality from the public sphere on the basis that "it is not of God," when in fact it simply isn't in line with their conception of God. We are *not* a Christian nation. We are not a Jewish, Muslim, or Hindu nation. We are not a Buddhist, Sufi, Baha'i, or any other officially religious nation. We are not an atheistic nation. We are a religiously pluralistic society in which one's freedom to worship as he or she wishes, or not to worship at all, is fully protected by law. Thomas Jefferson wrote in *Notes on the State of Virginia,* "It does me no injury for my neighbor to say there are twenty gods, or no god. It neither picks my pocket nor breaks my leg."

THERE are those in America today who seem to distrust the mechanics of liberty. Democracy is indeed a radical proposition. It is posited on the notion that each of us, from the depth of our own wisdom, brings to society the unique and precious gift of our own viewpoint and experience. We do not, and will not, always see things the same way; that is not a bad thing, but a good thing. Nowhere does this hold true more than in the area of religion.

In making a basic study of comparative religion—reading such books, for instance, as Huston Smith's *The World's Religions*—we see the universality of basic religious themes. Throughout the world, from Ireland to Bosnia to the Middle East, and increasingly in the United States, violence comes from fear born of ignorance of another's religious viewpoint. There is one God, and one God only. He pours Himself into many vessels, expressing His Truth in many ways, but still His Truth is one.

Our Founders did not wish to keep God out of the public sphere, but merely to make our society a place where He—or She, by the way—could be freely sought or not sought according to an individual's proclivity. Indeed, religious pluralism is a most crucial issue in the world today. We should be learning more about our own religious traditions *and* the traditions of our fellows. In this way we will come to know the unity in our religious diversity, without which we cannot appreciate the full genius of our American system of government or the greater glory of God.

RELIGION can be a confusing concept. The word itself comes from a root that means "to bind back." The actual religious experience is a "binding back" of our hearts to the truth within. An example of a spiritually based political force in America was the civil rights movement of the 1950s and 1960s. Although emanating from Martin Luther King's Southern Christian Leadership Conference, its call reached not only Christians but all people of goodwill, for its message was one of universal harmony and brotherhood. That's what made it so radical and also so purely religious. King's goal of achieving the "beloved community" is a vision at the heart of not one but all religious faiths.

There is an important distinction to be made between a religiously based and a spiritually based political impulse. While religion is a force that either creatively or noncreatively separates us, spirituality is a force that unites us by reminding us of our fundamental oneness. The religionization of American politics is dangerous; the spiritualization of our political consciousness is imperative.

When violence erupted in Israel in September of 1996 over the Israeli opening of a tunnel near the Dome of the Rock in Jerusalem, the clear difference between religious dogma and spiritual passion was obvious. For three of the great religions of the world, this particular piece of land is holy: Muslims believe that Muhammad ascended to heaven from there, the Jews believe that it is the spot from which God created the universe, and the Christians hold that Christ walked past there on his way to the cross. While a strictly exoteric religious perspective tempts us to compete for land, a genuine spiritual experience joins our hearts.

The authentic teachings of all the great religious perspectives reveal that it is not land that matters but love itself. God's call is not that we build His temple on a particular piece of land, but in our hearts. This is where the Rock is.

Many people in the world today use religion to divide us. They cite a particular book, whether the Bible, the Koran, or any other religious text, and claim that herein lies a universal prescription for all human behavior. Such fundamentalist mentality is more *about* God than *of* God, and the distinction between the two is one of the most important issues in world affairs today.

Of the People, By the People, For the People

America's first principles are inscribed not only in the Declaration of Independence and in our Constitution but also in Lincoln's Gettysburg Address. President Lincoln declared at Gettysburg that "this nation . . . shall have a new birth of freedom, and that government of the people, by the people, for the people, shall not perish from the earth." What a radical concept that is—a government of the people, by the people, for the people. It means, of course, that not only will the government consist of our citizens, elected by our citizens, but that its mission shall be to *serve* our citizens.

We should take a good look at that sentence—especially that part that reads "for the people"—and ask ourselves if we have decided to be the generation to repudiate Lincoln's words. President Rutherford B. Hayes once lamented that we were becoming a government "of the corporations, by the corporations, for the corporations." So what's new?

If ours were a government *for the people,* wouldn't our children receive the best education in the world? If ours were a government *for the people,* wouldn't we have universal health insurance? If ours were a government *for the people*, wouldn't we have massively committed to "clean" energy sources by now?

America's most fundamental problem is a crisis of our democratic process. We are being asked, as we were asked over two hundred years ago, to decide for ourselves and our children what it is worth to us to govern ourselves. While it appears that we have problems very different from those faced by earlier generations, in fact it is not the complexity of our current problems but rather the simple drama behind them all that should be garnering our attention. What we call the issues are not the issue. The issue is the disengagement of the average American's heart and mind from the democratic process. We have stopped participating in droves, and in our absence, forces not always in favor of the greatest good for the greatest number have exercised their own rights, often leaving the average American at a distinct disadvantage in our own country.

In 1864, Abraham Lincoln wrote these words:

> I see in the near future a crisis approaching that unnerves me and causes me to tremble for the safety of my country. As a result of the war, corporations have been enthroned and an era of corruption in high places will follow, and the money power of the country will endeavor to prolong its reign by working upon the prejudices of the people until all wealth is aggregated in a few hands and the Republic is destroyed.

The great issue of our time is not taxes, a balanced budget, social security or medicare. Those are all rather elaborate red herrings. The great issue that confronts us, as it confronted Jefferson's generation and Lincoln's generation and every generation to some degree, is this: Is America to be ruled *by* all of us and *for* all of us—or has the American government in fact become a government *of, by and for a relative few?*

A mean group of selfish people did not decide to steal America; what happened is that we gave her away. We have not been vigilant on behalf of our own good. We have failed to make periodic recourse to first democratic principles, allowing ourselves the disempowerment of ignorance and distraction. We have turned our eyes away from things that, in a free and democratic society, the citizenry cannot afford to turn our eyes away from.

Perhaps we are ready to turn them back.

Our Founders strove to overthrow the very notion of aristocracy, creating a system in which anyone could rise according to his or her own abilities, talents, and efforts. Jefferson thought democracy was humanity's best antidote for what he referred to as the "general prey of the rich on the poor"—*rebellion against which he considered natural and good.*

In a society where selfishness and greed have become the accepted ethos, a commitment to social justice is a rebellious mode of being. What is happening in America today is that there is not enough spirit of true rebellion. While a market-obsessed corporate mentality lords over us like a new ruling class, we act more like royalists than like our own Revolutionary forebears. This time we are not being assaulted directly, as the colonists were by the English through endless taxes and other burdens, but rather through an endless dripping stream of pleasure that the system is able to provide us, much like a low-grade morphine pump pushed into our veins, making us think we can't live without it. Pleasure can be used to enslave a person as effectively as pain.

And so, while we are not happy, perhaps we are having fun in some peculiar way or are so addicted to the pure adrenaline rush of contemporary culture that we no longer question the pain of it all. In short, we have fallen asleep.

One cannot dream the American Dream as long as one is sleeping. In order to dream the American Dream, the dreamer must be awake.

3

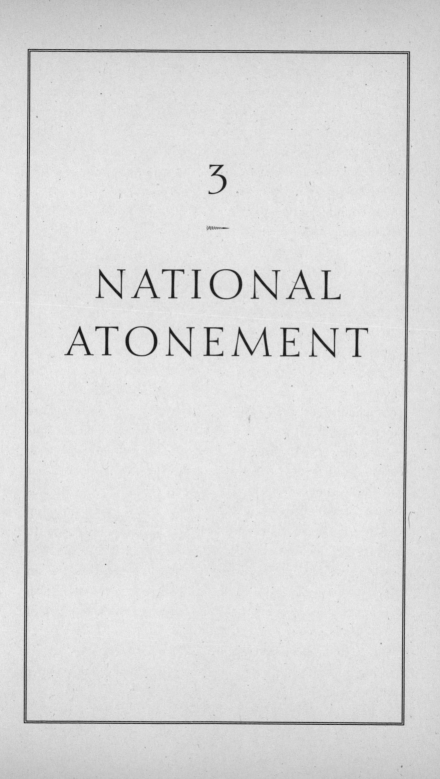

NATIONAL ATONEMENT

I n spiritual terms, the state of the soul is the awakened state, while the mortal personality dwells in perpetual sleep. That is why enlightened masters are often called the "awakened ones." Great souls—and all of us have a capacity for spiritual greatness, should our hearts be open wide enough—have the ability to see beyond personality, to the more spiritually "real" world than that of practical, worldly concerns.

Behind every human event is a spiritual drama, a deeper movement of the soul toward greater darkness or greater light. With every event, the soul either forgets itself or remembers itself, is either veiled by fear or shining forth in love. The individual life is a soul-drama, and so is the collective life of a nation, an ethnic group, a continent, and so on.

We have established already that the founding principles of the United States were a burst of light for all humanity. They form a system of liberty and justice, both of which are faces of the divine. But we have also established that, from our earliest days, the spiritual light of the United States has at times been eclipsed by the darkness of certain historical forces, many of which our Founders themselves had not outgrown. The march of modern civilization from its most primitive to its most evolved state—from the power of brute force to the power of soul force—is not a straight but a jagged line. Two steps forward, one step back, three steps sideways, and so goes history.

The plan of spiritual evolution is marked not only by God's will that we move ever in the direction of love, but also by another of God's creative principles: that humanity has free will. What that means is that in any given moment, it is our choice whether we move toward love or retreat from it. What is not love is fear. But in the larger scheme of things, there is a limit past which lovelessness cannot remain. Fear is not life-giving enough to sustain itself. We can move in the direction of fear only so long before it brings us to our knees, or to our end.

God is all-forgiving. He does not seek to judge and punish us, but to correct and heal us. He is not invested in our guilt but in our innocence. The spiritual principle by which He helps us return to love when we have strayed from its ways is the principle of Atonement.

The Atonement was introduced into human consciousness by God Himself, as a response to our capacity for fear. It is our eternal opportunity to choose again. That is what makes the Atonement a miracle: it is something introduced into the laws of time and space, by a power beyond them both. Grace supersedes the law of karma. To atone is to admit our errors, praying that God free us from what would otherwise be their inevitable consequences. It is a humble return of our minds to God's love. It is to recognize where we ourselves have taken a path away from God's will, and ask to be corrected and forgiven and healed. The story of the Prodigal Son makes clear how delighted God is when the son who strayed returns. By willingly and consciously unburdening ourselves of the weight of our mistakes, we are given the chance to begin again, to go forward in life from a healed perspective.

Could America not use a miracle?

The command to atone is a universal spiritual theme. In the

Jewish religion, Yom Kippur is the Day of Atonement, where Jews admit our errors of the past year, asking God's forgiveness and for His willingness to inscribe us in the Book of Life for another year. Catholics are called to confess their sins in regular confession. In Alcoholics Anonymous, "we admit to God, and to ourselves, the exact nature of our wrongs."

In an individual life, the importance of taking stock of *our own sins*—as opposed to indulging the ever-present temptation to catalogue someone else's—is a well-understood spiritual imperative. We cannot heal without it. And what of the life of a nation? Do we have collective sins to atone for as well? Is atonement part of our national healing?

Abraham Lincoln thought so. In proclaiming a National Day of Fasting and Prayer on March 30, 1863, Lincoln said,

> We have been preserved, these many years, in peace and prosperity. We have grown in numbers, wealth and power, as no other nation has ever grown. But we have forgotten God. We have forgotten the gracious hand which preserved us in peace, and multiplied and enriched and strengthened us; and we have vainly imagined, in the deceitfulness of our hearts, that all these blessings were produced by some superior wisdom of our own. Intoxicated with unbroken success, we have become too self-sufficient to feel the necessity of redeeming and preserving grace, too proud to pray to the God that made us!

He added,

> It behooves us, then, to humble ourselves before the offended Power, to confess our national sins, and to pray for clemency and forgiveness. It is the duty of nations as well as of men, to confess their sins and transgressions, in humble sorrow, yet with assured hope that genuine repentance will lead to mercy and pardon....

—

And what are America's sins or spiritual errors? Some are open to interpretation, of course, but some are clearly not. There are three main areas where America's need to atone weighs heavily on our national psyche: our cruel treatment, indeed genocide, of the Native American people; our racism toward African Americans throughout our history; and the terrible mistake that was the war in Vietnam.

A great nation, like a great person, is not one who has never fallen down, but one who has done what it takes to get back up. Once we're mature enough, we understand that there isn't one among us who has not made mistakes. The issue is not whether we have erred but, rather, what is God's attitude toward human errors? What would He have *our* attitudes be toward error in ourselves and others?

Atonement is the release from fear, not a dive deeper into it. It is a corrective device, not a punishment, to admit the exact nature of our wrongs and to do our best to make them right. Atonement is essential to the healing of the United States, because there will be no new America until we have done everything possible to right the wrongs of the old one.

Our nation, for many reasons, has developed a public personality that has great difficulty admitting when we have been wrong. Politicians, who ideally should be our primary healers, seem particularly loath to offend any voters by pointing out America's errors. This deeply obstructs our national healing because a collective, like an individual, simply cannot grow without taking responsibility for its own mistakes.

This clearly annoys other nations, which find our sometimes constant finger-wagging in their direction while refusing to admit our own transgressions the stuff of outrageous nerve. Even this, however, is secondary to the fact that, from a spiritual perspective, God Himself is not amused. "God shall not be mocked" means simply that He *isn't*.

What is our resistance to saying "We have been very, very wrong. We are sorry, and we apologize" in situations where it is so very clear that our capacity for error is as great as anyone else's? Are we afraid our children will find us weaker for doing so? Should we not rather be afraid that we are teaching them a false sense of strength—one that does not admit mistakes or humbly ask forgiveness? Should our children not know that, in fact, we are a great nation, with much to celebrate and be proud of, but that has also made mistakes and must ever be on guard against making them again?

Atonement is more than a mere apology. To atone is to do more than say you're sorry; it is to commit to *never do it again*. When we atone for past abuses toward someone, our prayer is that God remove whatever character defect within us led to the abuse to begin with, and transform us into someone not likely to repeat the error. And atonement includes the making of amends wherever and however possible.

Many people would say today, "Hey, *I* wasn't a slaveowner! It's not *my* responsibility!" or even "It's tragic what they did to the Indians, but hey, it's over." Yet the concept bears a closer look. Are these things really over? Doesn't the answer to that question have something to do with who you are and where you live? For poverty-stricken Indians living on reservations, or poverty-stricken African-American children living in the inner city, it could be argued that these situations *are not over*. The sins, or misperceptions, of the parents have been handed down to the children in successive generations, and while the original abuses no longer occur, they have "legs" that continue through the course of history. Contemporary poverty is the great-grandchild of abuses long past.

The abolition of slavery could be likened to the removal of a malignant tumor. The question for the doctor would not just be "Did you get out the tumor?" but "Did you get out all the cancer?" As long as there are any cancer cells left in the body, there is danger—because *cancer spreads.* An institution has been abolished, but the thinking that gave rise to it still lives. When it comes to slavery and racism, we got out the tumor but we didn't get out all the cancer.

To do that, it would help to apply the tenets of holistic healing. We must address the deeper causal issues involved in racial and ethnic tension today, and then apply the powers of body, mind, and spirit to bring forth the healing of our national wounds.

Forgiveness and Amends

Some people wish we were a color-blind society, but would that really be so wonderful? Homogenizing everyone so as to offend no one is hardly the way to true healing. It is both our unity *and* our diversity, after all, that underlies the American ideal. The only way we can become truly color-blind—that is, get to the point where we see each other only through the eyes of spirit, not even recognizing physical color—is if we first acknowledge the brilliance of the various colors.

Metaphysically, healing occurs when the darkness is brought to the light. You can't just say, "Okay, everybody. Let's love each other and pretend our colors don't exist, okay?" and then expect everything to be great. Not really. All that does is to force our issues down deeper, to impact them, and thus to ultimately exacerbate them. If you go to the doctor with a broken arm, you don't pretend you're there to heal your leg. The doctor says, "Let me take a look at that arm." And similarly, the divine physician says,

"Let me take a look at that wound in your psyche," not, "Let's ignore that wound." We need to show it to him, not cower from it.

President Clinton initiated a "national conversation" on race, certainly with the best of intentions. But that "conversation" has not as yet had deeper effects, because it is not as yet a deep conversation. It remains shallow, for the most part, because we are all too scared to get real, to be authentic, to tell it like it really is. Each of us is carrying around not only our own issues but also the issues of our parents and grandparents and their grandparents before them; like the adult children of alcoholic parents, we are living lives tainted by unprocessed feelings belonging to people long since gone. Psychologically, the United States is like a dysfunctional family system in which a huge "secret" goes undiscussed, breeding all manner of unconscious turmoil within various family members.

Within each of us, however, there is a reservoir of divine power that responds fully to our invitation to enter and restore us. Whether we call this force God, Christ, the Holy Spirit, the Jewish *shekina*, the Atman, the Oversoul, nonviolence, universal love, or whatever other words we wish, it is the all-powerful action of a "higher power." This power cannot work, however, counter to our free will; it must be invoked or consciously invited into our thought system. Then and only then can the atonement principle free us of the consequences of past mistakes.

As we make amends to those to whom we owe amends and try to forgive those who have hurt us, healing forces are released into the universe. Through atonement in the present, we both heal the past and release the future. As America atones for its mistakes, allowing itself the grief and sadness without which hearts cannot heal, love will replace the anger that underlies so much of our national life.

Metapolitical understanding takes us beyond a traditional understanding of our problems, and beyond a traditional set of solutions. That is why it is such an important new addition to our political awareness. Some problems take heart work, not just head work. All the laws in the world can't take a nation through its grieving or to its knees. Our wisdom will do that, or ultimately circumstances will. Those are our only two choices.

What is happening at the new millennium is that humanity is being challenged to bring our material realities into line with our emotional and spiritual realities. There are many uncried tears in this country, and every day we put off crying them, we simply create more tears for our children to cry later. Healing any area begins to heal them all.

DANCES WITH DEATH

Native Americans had lived on this continent for 1,000 generations before our European ancestors "discovered" it. The wisdom of the indigenous peoples of North America graced this soil for centuries before the white intruders arrived. It is estimated that in 1492 anywhere from 10 to 25 million indigenous people lived north of Mexico. Within 150 years, as a result of war and disease, there were fewer than a million Indians left here alive.

Part of the irony of the devastation of the Native American population by white expansion is that the Western world is now near the brink of global disaster because we lack contact with the very quality of consciousness that so many of the Indian people personified. We killed them, and now we need them. How much better off America would be today had our ancestors been wise enough to take advantage, on a mass level, of the extraordinary opportunity presented to them to marry European and Native American cultures. Using anthropologist Riane Eisler's terms in her landmark book *The Chalice and the Blade,* they opted for the dominator rather than partnership model of human development. That was characteristic of the historical era now closing, but hopefully not of the one now being born.

Americans love cowboys. We've embraced the myth of the brave pioneer, the explorer of strange lands, the conquerer of unexpected dangers. There's an upside to that from which clearly we were born as a nation. But the myth has a darkside as well, and processing that myth is critical to our healing. Once again, the yang is extraordinary, but woe the absence of yin, of feeling and understanding. Whether the explorer/cowboy/pioneer we embrace is Christopher Columbus sailing to America, Buffalo Bill riding out West, or a modern CEO of a multinational corporation expanding into communities and nations around the globe, it should not be forgotten that that figure, despite his courage and self-sufficiency, is an *outlaw*. He is not known for his respect for other people, his honor of those who got there first, or his willingness to leave well enough alone when told that he can't have his way.

The way consciousness operates is that a myth represents a part of ourselves. If we applaud in a myth what should not be applauded, then (1) we are stuck at that place within ourselves, and (2) we are at the *effect* of that place within ourselves. The price we pay for admiring the conquerer is that we will inevitably be conquered. The universe will make sure of it; it's an area where we have something to learn.

Demythologizing this figure, removing him (or her) from his pedestal in our imagination, will help free us from his dominion. Often our approval, and our healing, begins on a symbolic level. Our glorification of Christopher Columbus, for instance, is a mythological distortion, and repealing Columbus Day would be a move in the direction of national healing. For all the fiction created around him, Columbus was a murderer of indigenous peoples, and exalting him is a symbol of our neurotic attraction to violent outlaws. At our current stage of development, if someone violates one person, we can see that the person is a criminal. But if the individual violates many, the sheer power involved can appear sexy. Part of our evolution involves healing our deadly unconscious connection between brute force and sexuality. It is at the core of humanity's problems, as evidenced by our national as well as personal politics. Once again, if just one person attacks another, it's obviously horrible. But if a nation attacks another nation—*and the attacking nation happens to be us*—then all too often it's a reason to have a drink and celebrate.

Given the fact that Columbus's life was a model for the standard of enslavement and killing that came to characterize much of European settlement in the New World, to honor him is deeply insulting to our Native American brothers and sisters. Moreover, it stunts the collective psyche of the nation that we are so dishonest about our history.

In 1992, at the time of the quincentennial celebration of his "discovery" of America, there was a national rethinking of Columbus's appropriate place in history. The National Council of Churches, the largest ecumenical body in the United States, called on Christians to refrain from celebrating the quincentennial, saying, "What represented newness of freedom, hope, and opportunity for some was the occasion for oppression, degradation, and genocide for others." When it comes to celebrating Columbus or Columbus Day, we should *just say no.*

I have watched with interest New York City's efforts to clean up Columbus Circle; it seems like it just can't be done. Although the intersection of Central Park South and Central Park West should be one of Manhattan's most exciting points, that circle has a seedy energy that, like the blood on Lady Macbeth's hands, doesn't ever seem to wash away. No matter how many times they sandblast that statue, you never really want to look at it. And no matter how many ways they try to dress up that entrance to Central Park, it continues to be a questionable location. There's only one way to clean up Columbus Circle: take the statue down and rename the place. It's a moral black hole.

I have heard people acknowledge that Columbus himself poses a problem, yet they wouldn't want to give up Columbus Day as a holiday because it celebrates the contributions of Italians to American civilization. If what we are excited about, and indeed we should be, is how many people from other lands have enriched America, then perhaps we could change Columbus Day to Immigrant's Day. I realize how many people would not want *that*, of course—but maybe that is all the more reason we should propose it.

We are not so much undereducated regarding Native American history in this country as we are wrongly educated. For better or for worse, we are taught as much by television and movies as we are by textbooks, and in both cases, we have been fed misleading stereotypes regarding the "Cowboy and Indian" days. There was nothing romantic about that era from the Native American point of view. By the late 1800s, there was little left to do but clean up the mess after centuries of the white European's complete devastation of the indigenous American culture. The Indians by then were finished as a major civilization; their numbers were decimated and their cultural subjugation was nearly complete.

Brutish behavior toward Native Americans had started centuries before, but that behavior was codified into American law in the nineteenth century. In 1830, the U.S. Congress passed the Indian Removal Act, paving the way for the forced relocation of the Cherokee nation. What followed was an intense political controversy, in which many brave Americans—including the celebrated Tennessee Senator David Crockett—stood up for conscience against the injustice of the U.S. policy toward Native Americans. His words ring powerfully through the air today: "I would sooner be honestly damned than hypocritically immortalized." Alas, however, he spoke them to no avail.

In his book *Don't Know Much About History,* author Kenneth C. Davis writes:

> Early in the summer of 1832, General Scott and the United States Army began the invasion of the Cherokee Nation.
>
> In one of the saddest episodes of our brief history, men, women and children were taken from their land, herded into makeshift forts with minimal facilities and food, then forced to march a thousand miles (Some made part of the trip by boat in equally horrible conditions).... About 4,000 Cherokee died as a result of the removal. The route they traversed and the journey itself became known as "The Trail of Tears" or, as a direct translation from Cherokee, "The Trail Where They Cried"....
>
> And so a country formed fifty years earlier on the premise "that all men are created equal, and that they are endowed by their Creator with certain inalienable rights, among these the right to life, liberty and the pursuit of happiness" brutally closed the curtain on a culture that had done no wrong.

While the Trail of Tears is the most dramatic single example of our nation's violent behavior toward Native Americans, it was unfortunately part of a much larger historical pattern. What might have been a most glorious cultural partnership—we should remember how many Native Americans graciously welcomed their new white "friends" from across the ocean—became instead the most debased domination of one culture by another. It is left to us to atone for past errors, and seek to redress them.

While in some cases in our history it was death to the Indians, in others it was merely death to their culture. "Helping" people become "more like us" is more oppression than liberation unless those people want to! And in so many cases, why would they? Native Americans could see, long before we did, the spiritual errors of the white man's way, the insane brutality of an order that made the word *bigger* more important than the word *good*, and that values outer power over internal wisdom.

While the majority of Native Americans had sought to live peacefully with the white man, their proffers of peace had been met by murder, enslavement, and land theft. The basic suppression of Native American culture became an entrenched cultural phenomenon in America that continues to this day.

Throughout this century, American Indians have been the poorest of the poor in American society. In the early 1900s, American Indians were concentrated in remote regions of the nation, distant from urban centers of economic growth. From 1890 to 1930, the federal government's so-called allotment programs vigorously promoted farming as a means for American Indians to become self-sufficient, but the farmland they were allotted was often arid and of poor quality. In some areas, many tribes were former nomadic hunters and had neither the knowledge nor the desire to become farmers. The history of this period is replete with examples of the most egregious violations of Indian rights.

After forty years, during which time Indians had failed to become self-sufficient, President Roosevelt created the Indian New Deal, trying to help reservations deal with the economic hardship created by the Great Depression. With the outbreak of World War II, however, the Indian New Deal was cut short and a new set of policies—"termination" and "relocation"—were designed to dissolve reservations and resettle American Indians to urban areas. Between 1952 and 1972, more than 100,000 American Indians were relocated to cities, under the belief, illusion, or pretext that exposure to urban labor markets would improve their standard of living. However, Indians often lacked the education, skills, and experience to find employment and benefit from such relocation.

Since the early 1970s, the federal government has adopted a policy of "self-determination" that has allowed American Indians to be more involved in issues affecting their reservations. Native American leaders have taken a variety of steps to increase economic activity, and many of the reservations are endowed with natural resources such as timber, minerals, and water. During the 1980s, many tribes established gambling operations, which have been lucrative for many, though understandably controversial.

I am not a Native American, and so I can hardly speak for the Indian soul. But words like *relocation* are chilling to me. Forcing people who once roamed free and magnificently over lands they had called theirs for thousands of years, into little areas that we deemed unworthy of us and therefore good enough for them, or into the brash, clankering maze of urban society on the pretense that "maybe they can find jobs there," is culturally, spiritually, emotionally, and psychologically criminal. It warrants the grief and tears not only of Native Americans but also of all people of conscience and goodwill. Native American culture is not market based, but spirit based; that is not its primitivism but its sophistication. The sacred nature of *all* things is deemed far more important than the economic value of *anything*. *We* are the barbarians.

Little we have done can heal the collective wound on the soul of the Sioux, the Navajo, the Cherokee, and others—peoples who bear the legacy of one of the most spiritually advanced races of people, now diminished in both stature and freedom. Today's rates of alcoholism, poverty, and depression within the Native American community are understandable tragedies given the historical circumstances from which they stem.

If we're interested in healing our national soul, we will officially atone to the Native American culture and its people. Have things gotten better for Native Americans during the last few years? In some ways, many people would say yes. Yet notice that even improvement is measured by the grossest of materialistic standards: the sheer ability to survive.

In the last three decades, there has been a growing renaissance of regard for the genius of Native American culture. Hopefully, this will increase awareness among all Americans, not only of the debt we owe to Native Americans for what they gave to us but also for what was done *to* them as a result of the white man's expansion westward. Indians themselves have been having a good long cry for the last three hundred years; when our hearts are touched by the tragedy of Native American history, by the obliteration of practically an entire civilization, then surely we, too, will cry. Americans need a good cry over things such as this. Our apparent insensitivity to the sufferings of people "not like us" is a national character defect, a part of our political personality unworthy of who we really are. If one suffering child, of any color, were to be placed in front of the average American, I believe that that American would care and act to assuage the suffering. But there is something about *lots* of people suffering that, quite counterintuitively, makes Americans tune out instead of tune in. Awareness of our tendency to deny what is too difficult to face— and asking God to heal us of this collective defect and wound— is part of our path to higher consciousness and ultimately our national healing.

Dear God,
Please forgive us our grievous errors.
We atone and ask forgiveness for
our early treatment of the indigenous people,
the natives of the North American continent,
who suffered devastation at the hands of our forefathers.
We atone and ask forgiveness for

the places where we dishonor them still.
Help us, Lord,
so mend our thoughts that we no longer
rebel against Your Spirit, which is Love.
Forgive us now.
Turn our darkness into light, dear God,
through Your power which does these things,
that we might awaken to a new America.
May hatred be replaced by love here,
and true justice prevail at last.
May we meet each other in reborn brotherhood,
and begin again in love.
Dear Lord,
Please compensate for the injustices done
unto the Native American peoples,
and use us to bring forth new good.
We atone for the past,
and ask that our hearts be opened now.
Dear God,
Please restore what has been harmed
and heal us all.
To our Native American brothers and sisters, we say:
Please forgive us
for the evils that have been perpetrated
against your people
in the name of the United States.
At last,
May the spirit of your ancestors
Shine joyfully in your children.
Forgive us, God.
Amen

RACIAL ATONEMENT

The United States is like a torch that has, in various chapters of our history, both enlightened the world and burned the world.

A wound very much alive in America is the tortured relationship between blacks and whites. For this, atonement is only the beginning of what is morally demanded of us. "I tremble for my country," wrote Thomas Jefferson, "when I consider God is just, and that His justice shall not sleep forever." With the abolition of slavery we began the road to political justice, and with the civil rights movement we continued it. The largest underlying conflict regarding racial tension in America today is between those who essentially believe that we've done enough—that we've created a just society for African Americans—and those who believe we have only just begun, that we're still early in the process of making true amends for the evils of slavery.

Thought is the causal level of the universe. In abolishing slavery, we did not abolish racist thinking. Indeed, such societies as the Ku Klux Klan were founded after the end of the Civil War, in direct response to the abolition of slavery. While external legislative remedies are an aid to racial healing, spiritual forces are necessary to heal the terrible wounds to the heart and soul. Cellular memory of hatred and abuse has accumulated among African Americans to such an extent that it has become a generational resentment, leaving only two choices on the road ahead: the relationship between our races will turn to violence unless it turns to love.

The only way our "national conversation on race" will be a meaningful one is if white America acknowledges its culpability in institutionalizing racism, including formalized amends to the African-American people, and if black America receives a deep and serious invitation to voice its frustrations in a dignified way, one that honors the depth of injury and insult to African-American people throughout our history.

Many white people have expressed dismay that now, when in some ways we have indeed made real strides in the civil rights arena, more blacks who have fared well seem to be expressing increased anger. But psychologically this makes sense: once your stomach is full, you have more time to think. "Black rage" is an accumulated response to generation after generation of insult. It's not just what people have experienced but also what their parents and parents' parents experienced that often moves through their veins and erupts like hot oil. At the end of the millennium, an unconscious message is breaking through from all marginalized people: "Enough is enough." That message isn't going to be getting any quieter.

One in three black Americans lives in poverty—three times the rate of whites. Half of all black children in America live in poverty. Unemployment for African Americans is twice as high as it is for whites, and has been for the last thirty years. For the same educational background blacks can expect to make 82 to 86 percent of the income of whites. Economic injustice toward blacks in America is a systemically racist phenomenon, and to minimize it is further racism. When blacks understandably object to their own oppression, they're liable to be told in one way or another: "There you go—complaining again!"

People who haven't been listened to for over two hundred years have a lot to process. All over the country, people are gathering in racial healing circles to talk out these issues, pray for reconciliation, and seek the power of genuine forgiveness.

On May 16, 1997, President Clinton offered a public apology on behalf of the nation to the victims of the federal government's Tuskegee Study of Untreated Syphilis in the Negro Male, an infamous chapter in the history of American medical research. In that study, starting in 1932, 399 indigent black men from

Tuskegee, Alabama, were told that they would receive free medical treatment for syphilis, but instead were left untreated and carefully monitored. Even after penicillin was found to be a successful cure in the mid-1940s, the men were left untreated. "To our African-American citizens, I am sorry that your Federal Government orchestrated a study so clearly racist," said the President. The government, said President Clinton, "did something that was wrong—deeply, profoundly, morally wrong. It was an outrage to our commitment to integrity and equality for all our citizens."

It is very heartening to hear the President make that statement, but it is also very important that we not use our apologies for specific instances of racism to help us ignore the larger issue of our society's debt to a long-enslaved people. It is not enough to treat the symptoms of racism; we must treat the disease itself. Tuskegee was part of a larger pattern of abuse that stemmed from a general feeling that the lives of black people do not deserve the same respect and consideration as the lives of white people. President Clinton's action was a good beginning—nothing more and nothing less. I hope it will help us open our eyes to the plight of millions of black children today, whose diseases of poverty, ignorance, and substandard medical care are going every bit as dangerously untreated as was syphilis in Tuskegee sixty-five years ago. The bigger problem is far from behind us.

I do not believe the average American is racist, but I believe the average American does not truly realize how tilted our public resources are away from America's black communities and in the direction of America's richer white citizens. Although the Emancipation of the slaves gave African Americans their political freedom, their bondage was replaced by a more subtle but equally oppressive form of slavery: an economic slavery that continues to this day. Lack of educational opportunities, lack of job training, lack of economic revitalization measures, lack of mass transit, and lack of adequate housing among poor segments of the African-American population are all examples of white America's failure to pay one of its most important debts. In fact—and this is the larger issue—we do not have in America today a consensus that there is even a debt to be paid.

What is this in our national temperament? Why is it that we resist the recognition of the tremendous moral debt we owe to a people brought here against their will and enslaved for centuries? Are we afraid that our feelings of guilt, were they to be authentically owned, would overwhelm us? Why are we avoiding what any individual knows: that cleaning up the past is a prerequisite for a fruitful future? Why is it that even a Congressional *apology* is too much to ask?

After the Civil War ended, America's former slaves were just left on their own to try to make lives for themselves. Given the historical circumstances of that time, one can understand why abolition itself seemed such an extraordinary thing—which it was. But while many of the descendants of slaves have clearly forged lives of triumph and abundance, millions more now pack the inner cities of the United States. For them, the trauma is far from over. Those neighborhoods are, in many ways, our slave quarters.

In these communities today, social and economic conditions are often as harrowing as those of the worst days of the Great Depression. And these current conditions have been occuring for thirty years, while the Depression lasted ten years. We considered the Depression a catastrophe, and wouldn't have dreamed of the government *not* trying to help lift people out of their poverty. Today, one is reminded of the words of Dr. King, "If it happens to white people, they call it a Depression. If it happens to black people, they call it a social problem."

An apology is the yin we need, and serious restitution is the yang. When African Americans say the word *reparations*, you'd think they had suggested something completely outrageous. But the general concept is legitimate. Germany paid somewhere around $50 billion in restitution to Jews after World War II. The United States paid $20,000 to every Japanese American who had been sent to a concentration camp here in America during World War II. Nothing short of a massive investment in America's poor black population—the true legacy of slavery—is a responsible sign of America's willingness to heal itself racially. The most depressed communities in America, which are primarily African American, cry out for help, and we act like it's some major liberal coup every time we even throw them a crumb.

After World War II, the United States spent $12 billion over four years on the Marshall Plan, rebuilding the devastated economies of Western Europe. Why would we be less generous to citizens of the United States?

When I have said to friends, "Why don't we take $100 billion over the next ten years, and spend $10 billion a year to rebuild our inner cities?", I've usually been met with lines like, "Oh, but that's so much money! Where would we get the money?" Then I mention that we spend $271 billion every year on our military budget, $30 billion every year on the CIA, and more than $100 billion each year on corporate subsidies. All of a sudden $10 billion to *help* people doesn't seem like such an insane idea.

We need rituals of atonement and apology for American racism, past and present. I have experienced such prayers, and their healing power is profound. But we also need to make a serious and honorable amends, in the form of substantial efforts to economically revitalize a segment of our population that happens to be poor and happens to be black. Why should our national attitudes be so punitive rather than loving? Dr. King said that the American Congress was much less compassionate than the American people, and I think that is true today. We are a better nation than this. If we will devote the next ten years of our history to turning this area of national shame into an area of national atonement, the gift to our children and our children's children—*all* our children—will be immeasurable.

AN apology is so important because, without it, there is no real atonement. It releases the emotional truth of a situation. Certain Americans think that blacks just need to forgive slavery and move on with their lives—but isn't it easier to forgive someone when he or she has had the courtesy to apologize?

A sincere apology is more than just "emotional symbolism," to quote Newt Gingrich on the idea of a Congressional apology. An apology is an act of atonement, and only in a society that trivializes faith is atonement viewed as mere symbol.

Faith, for those of us who embrace it, is as *real* as a car, a house, or a piece of legislation. The power of God in our lives is no less *real* than technology, business, or sports. The fact that the action of faith is invisible to the physical eye does not make it a mere function of our imagination or a metaphor or psychological child's play. A national apology, performed sincerely from the hearts of white Americans, would carry tremendous power because it would affect our collective consciousness. The hand of God would come upon us.

The trivialization of faith by the political status quo—from the Left with its rolled eyes, to the Right with its hypocritical words of support—has created a huge void in the center of American political consciousness. Faith in God is not faith in a particular religious dogma. Faith in God is faith in love, faith in a higher power, and ultimately faith in each other. Atonement means turning back the darkness through a prayerful embrace of the light.

Human beings, on the level of spirit, are not separate but joined as one. In the words of Dr. King, "We are all caught in an inescapable network of mutuality." The reason the Golden Rule is essential to all religious thought is that what we do to others *will* be done to us, and if not to us then to our children or our children's children. We *will* reap what we sow, and what we withhold from others *will* be withheld from us. Time itself is a trick of the mind. We must give justly, not merely because we're "good" but because we understand cosmic law. It is no longer possible to be realistically satisfied with our own circumstances if the opportunities for the same abundance are unfairly denied to others. The day of reckoning—a kind of instant karma—is at hand.

The black poor in America can be likened to a patient bleeding to death in an emergency room. One side of the political spectrum says, "Let's do nothing for him. It's a free country and he could walk out of the emergency room if he wanted to. He's probably faking this illness anyway." Another side says, "Let's give him a manicure while he's lying here. Perhaps it will make him feel better. If he's still weak after that, let's be modern about this and give him some vitamin C." Add to that the fact that he is bleeding to death because of a congenital disease he inherited from his father, who got it from his father, who got it from his father, whose father got the disease through injection from *us.*

There are those who would point to blacks who have behaved criminally or dysfunctionally, and try to use that as justification for not performing our ethical duty to the African-American community. Or, conversely, one can point to black stars who have triumphed, and try to claim that because they made it big in America, that proves there's no real problem. But neither argument is valid. Every group of people has its shadow element, and every group has its geniuses. Neither is an excuse for failing to live up to our moral obligations. America has a *huge*—not a nonexistent, not a small, nor even a medium-sized—problem on its hands. We should see this for what it is and act accordingly.

When it comes to institutionalized systems of racial injustice, there is a myth in the United States that what has merely lessened has in fact ended. White America has not yet given up our collective attitude, however covert, that we are a superior race and culture. While there are many millions of people to whom this attitude truly does not apply, it continues to permeate our social, political, and economic policies. God does not love anyone more than He loves anyone else, and His universe will not endlessly tolerate an attitude on the part of white-skinned people that we have, for any reason whatsoever, greater right than others do to the opportunities afforded us by this great land. It is astonishing to me that a culture that mass-murdered Native Americans and brought millions of Africans here to be slaves has the audacity to still say to those and those like them, "Be careful not to get in our way."

Psychologically, we are subconsciously afraid of those whom we have wronged. We are afraid that they will punish us, as we secretly feel we deserve to be punished. I believe that this psychological dynamic is at the core of much of white America's attitude toward African Americans. We are afraid to truly share power with blacks because we are afraid of what they might do with such power if they had it. We are afraid that they might treat us as we have treated them.

Meanwhile, with this attitude—however unconscious on our part—we perpetuate the very forces that would make anyone angry, thus adding to the already raging fire that burns within so many hearts.

In a reborn America, there is going to be the most amazing, blazing light emanating from black culture. There is a profound spiritual authority among those who have already forgiven us, in spite of the fact that we have not yet even asked forgiveness. It is particularly prevalent among certain black women, and it is one of the sacred spots on the American psychic landscape. The day will come when we will see things with our spiritual eyes, and when we do, we will stand in awe before the power of this love. It is a big love. It is a blessing on us all. It does more to keep this country from exploding than any of us will ever know.

THESE WORDS of Robert Kennedy resonate today:

> I urge you to learn the harsh facts that lurk behind the mask of official illusion with which we have concealed our true circumstances, even from ourselves. Our country is in danger: Not just from foreign enemies; but above all, from our own misguided policies, and what they can do to this country. There is a contest, not for the rule of America, but for the heart of America.

The universe will compensate us royally if we do what it takes to truly right the spiritual course of this nation. White America will not lose money or power if it pays off its moral debts: The whole country will become richer and more powerful beyond our wildest imaginations. We will take a quantum leap forward as a nation if we embrace the opportunity before us and genuinely atone.

"The holiest of all the spots on earth," according to *A Course in Miracles,* "is where an ancient hatred has become a present love." Let us imagine the glory that could be, and pray to bring it forth.

> Dear God,
> Please forgive us for the evils of slavery,
> racism and injustice.
> Please heal, dear Lord,
> our hardened hearts.
> We atone to God,
> And ask forgiveness of the African-American people,
> For the slavery in both body and spirit

of your men, your women and your children.
To you who have lived among us,
and suffered the sting of our unfair dominion—
For the abuse of both your ancestors
And your children,
We pray for the absolution of the Lord.
We ask that God restore us all,
and use us as His instruments
for the resurrection of good.
We deeply apologize for the errors of the past
and ask that America's heart be opened now.
If we could rewrite history,
We would.
We cannot,
but God can.
Dear God, please do.
To the African-American community,
We acknowledge the tears of your people,
the suffering of your ancestors,
and the brilliance of your culture.
We bless your children,
Please bless ours.
May God in His glory
Forge a brotherhood between us,
For brothers indeed
we are.
Dear God,
Please send a miracle.
Amen

THE LESSONS OF VIETNAM

One of the reasons we need to atone for our treatment of both
Native Americans and black Americans is that it will help us
break the chain with that part of our national character that still

wants to grab for what it wants in the world, without regard to the life or livelihood of others.

Robert McNamara, who was President Johnson's Secretary of Defense during the Vietnam War, has written in his memoirs that the war was "a terrible mistake." More than 59,000 Americans dead, plus countless other devastated lives, and it was all "a terrible mistake." McNamara also mentioned that he, and others who planned and directed that war, had no knowledge or understanding of the religion, language, philosophy, or character of the people of Vietnam—and no one to teach them, even if they wanted to learn.

After hearing that, if we were an enlightened society, we would all have gone to bed for three days. We would cry, moan, get sick, scream it out, punch punching bags, do whatever it takes to get the pain up and out of our cells. There is an inestimable human tragedy stuck to this nation as a result of that war, a significant aspect of which is the ever-more-frayed bond of trust between the American people and our government.

The Vietnam War Memorial is a uniquely powerful place because it is emotionally true. It doesn't lie. It pictures the war as a huge black gash across our landscape, which it is. It appropriately memorializes the lives of those who died such purposeless, tragic deaths in Vietnam. And it helps us grieve not only for them but also for who we were as a nation before that war so wounded us.

At a traveling exhibit of the Vietnam Wall, I saw the following letter posted by an ex-Marine. It reveals more truth about that war than most history books do.

> On the Second of July 1967, Alpha and Bravo companies of the First Battalion, Ninth Marines were on patrol just a few hundred meters south of the DMZ.
>
> Bravo blundered into a well-set ambush at the marketplace; soon, Alpha, too, was in the thick of it.

———

The enemy consisted of a regiment of the North Vietnamese Army supported by artillery, heavy mortars, rockets, anti-aircraft guns, and surface-to-air missiles.

Charlie and Delta companies were rushed to the field in support, but the outcome had been decided. The Marines were overwhelmingly outnumbered.

But, worse than that, they were equipped with Colt M-16 rifles. Their M-14 rifles, which had proven so effective and reliable, were stored in warehouses, somewhere in the rear.

The M-16s would fire once or twice—maybe more—then jam. The extractor would rip the rim off the casing. Then the only way to clear the chamber and resume firing was to lock open the bolt, run a cleaning rod down the barrel, and knock the casing loose. Soon it would jam again.

This was the rifle supplied to her troops by the richest nation on earth. The enemy was not so encumbered. They carried rifles that were designed in the Soviet Union and manufactured in one of the poorest nations on earth—the so-called People's Republic of China. Their rifles fired. Fired every time. They ran amongst the Marines, firing at will.

Sixty-four men in Bravo were killed that afternoon. Altogether, the Battalion lost around a hundred of the nation's finest men. The next morning, we bagged them like groceries. We consigned their bodies to their families and commended their souls to God. May He be as merciful as they were courageous.

Today, people are still debating the issue: Was it the fault of the ammo? The fault of the rifle? Neither. It was the fault of the politicians and contractors and generals. People in high places knew the rifles and ammo wouldn't work together. The military didn't want to buy the rifle when Armalite was manufacturing it. But when Colt was licensed as the manufacturer, they suddenly discovered it was a marvelous example of Yankee ingenuity.

Sgt. Brown told them it was garbage. Col. Hackworth told them it was garbage. And every real Grunt knew it was garbage. It was unsuited for combat.

There was no congressional investigation. No contractor was ever fined for supplying defective material. No one uncovered the bribes paid to government officials. No one went to jail. And the mothers of dead Marines were never told that their sons went into combat unarmed.

To all outward appearances, those Marines died of gunshot and fragmentation wounds. But a closer examination reveals that they were first stabbed in the back by their countrymen.

The politicians, contractors, and generals have retired to comfortable estates now. Their ranks have been filled by their clones—greedy invertebrates every one. They should hope that God is more forgiving than I.

Brave men should never be commanded by cowards.

First Lieutenant Harvey G. Wysong
0100308
United States Marine Corps Reserve
First Battalion, Nine Marines

It was not just Johnson and McNamara who made a terrible mistake in Vietnam: The entire nation made a terrible mistake in letting them do it. One would think that, after such a debacle, America would no longer allow those in power, in uniform, in "command," to so easily make absurd decisions on our behalf. And yet we do. What a tragedy, all that false respect we had— and still have—for the trappings and illusions of worldly power. We still have not opened ourselves collectively to the shame and horror of that huge mistake. We have not atoned to our vets, to their families, to God, to other nations involved, or to ourselves. Until we do, we shall remain in some way under the effect of that mistake. Even worse, we will continue to repeat it.

Perhaps we are repeating it now.

We need a miracle of God to remove from us our almost pathological attachment to the twisted romance of the military.

Our attitudes in this area, judging from our military budget and behavior, are no more enlightened today than they were thirty years ago. Our increasing militarism is part of our ever more appalling culture of violence.

God help us.

> Dear God,
> Please forgive us
> For the war in Vietnam.
> We deeply apologize
> To that nation,
> And to our own.
> To their people,
> And to our own.
> To our veterans:
> To the spirits of those who died there,
> May you rest in peace.
> To those who were sent there and survived,
> May you be restored.
> To those of you who lost your loved ones,
> May you find peace.
> Dear God,
> Please remove from this nation
> Our militaristic illusions,
> Our temptation
> To see more power in hatred
> Than power in love,
> And to believe the lies
> Of a war machine
> Before the truth
> In our hearts.
> Dear God,
> Please forgive us
> For our violation of any nation
> Toward whom we have done wrong.

> Please lift us up.
> Please heal this wound.
> Amen

To heal ourselves, we must grieve our past.

You cannot dedicate a nation to the high ideals to which this one was dedicated and not expect the soul to rebel in some way when you start acting as if you didn't really mean it.

From the genocide of Native Americans to our systematic racism to the Vietnam War, the United States needs, as they say in the twelve-step recovery program, to take a "fearless moral inventory." We are not to spend the rest of our lives in an endless string of *mea culpas,* but as soon as we say at least a few sincere ones, the miracle of atonement will begin to release our collective soul.

God is merciful. I do not believe He is angry, but He's not kidding either. He has asked us to love each other, as He so loves us. And to Him, these are not just words.

4

AN AMERICAN AWAKENING

M o s t people I know who are interested in the word *healing* do not particularly like the word *politics*. *Healing* implies to them something loving, organic and soulful, while *politics* implies something fear based, power addicted, and brutish.

For years we have been pouring our most creative thinking into the building of new paradigm models—in education, health, business, relationships. Yet politics has seemed so dirty, we haven't even wanted to deal with the subject. Now that is changing. Even if we don't perceive politics as the most powerful vehicle for positive change—and from a spiritual perspective, it clearly isn't—who can deny how destructive it can be when dominated by the thoughts of fear and shame?

The problem is not politics per se, but rather an evil we sense lurking in its house. Evil wears a business suit in the world today, hiding behind pinstripes, smiling away. Our biggest problem is not a person or an institution, but a worldview that threatens to destroy all things. It is a sensibility—a sleazy, seductive way of seeing the world—that has no human conscience nor concern for the future. *The enemy, of course, is America's false god, our new bottom line, our economic obsessiveness.* It is literally beastly, as it would gobble up our children, our planet, our freedom itself, to satisfy its appetite for endless control. While it clearly has a stronghold in American politics, its goal is to dominate the world.

This problem has become like an inoperable, hidden cancer—always lurking behind this or that, a spider tumor whose root inside you seems impossible to rout out. It is a cancer underlying all our cancers; it is spiritual and systemic, and cannot be treated effectively through any traditional means.

There is no one to be angry at, for we are all conspirators in some way or the other. The only way to defeat the enemy is to collectively rise above it. There is no silver bullet for this problem, nor pat political solution. It is not a medicine we need, but a healing process. The problem is an opportunistic infection that would not have occurred, had the citizenry of the United States not given up its social immune system function in the American body politic.

Yet how do we create a new politics—a forcefield of citizens engaged enough to repudiate the spectral threat in our midst—particularly at a time when the old one is so smugly sure of itself, so bolstered by gargantuan material power? The answer is, with spiritual perspicacity. We don't have to worry about what's happening now; the heartless falls of its own dead weight. Our economic and political status quo will pass into oblivion, as it represents a state of spiritual sleep. Our task is not to fight it; our task is to ourselves wake up.

THE most critical metapolitical issue in America today is the numbing and suppression of personal power within the individual American citizen. Political power ultimately derives from the personal confidence and courage to express oneself. Where a social system has failed to adequately educate its citizens, has bombarded our nervous systems with an overstimulation of mindless entertainment, has promoted consumerism as the primary social activity, and has accepted the numbing of the resultant pain with massive use of antidepressants as a substitute for questioning the pain itself, personal power becomes the purview of a lucky or courageous few. The game of the culture has been to respond to our feelings of disempowerment by exploiting those very feelings—trying to convince us that if we buy this or that product, or elect this or that official, our feelings of well-being will be miraculously restored.

Americans as individuals tend to be spunky and eminently decent. We are great to sit next to on airplanes. As a group, however, we have a capacity for denial and grandiosity that makes us increasingly easy targets for manipulation by the media, politicians, or false advertising campaigns. We have become completely taken in by the business of public relations.

Much of our education was training in passive acceptance of someone else's perspective rather than development of the ability to create our own; television has all but destroyed our capacity for critical thinking; our linear thought processes are jumbled like crackling cereal; and we are left with a dangerous propensity to be taken for a ride by anyone who can afford a specialist at scrambling our brains even more.

We have been lulled to sleep by an official culture that speaks nonsense to us as though it were reasonable and have been trained since childhood by a consumer culture to conspire in our own psychological bondage. The lullabies are compelling, but waking up is better.

As we meditate and pray, we begin to awaken. As we read good books, we begin to awaken. As we eschew bad television, we begin to awaken. As we serve our community, we begin to awaken. As we journey toward psychological health, we begin to awaken. As we think for ourselves, we begin to awaken. As we communicate more freely, we begin to awaken. As we take up the philosophical mantle of concern for the future of life on earth, and apply it as best we can to our social, professional, and political endeavors, we begin to awaken ourselves and others. And in that awakening lies hope for all of us. Mass awakening from our entrenched delusions is the only hope for America's healing.

Iᴛ s not an accident that Americans have become so passive in the face of systemic threats to our freedom. For decades, the American public education system tried to teach children *what* to think, avoiding its greater mission in a free society: to teach children *how* to think. Teaching children how to think means fostering minds that are questioning, assertive, open-minded, and creative. We should bring up our children to be creators, not imitators, for only that prepares them for the wonder of life.

That is an outlook that the perpetuation of democracy requires, but that an industrialized economic system came more and more to resist. While we were dominated economically by the rule of industrialization, the tacit pact that American education made with industry was to provide the system with masses of Americans who would show up on time, do as they were told, not ask a lot of questions, and not bother to assert themselves.

A child would enter kindergarten excited and passionate. By the sixth grade at the latest, his or her passion was squelched. Passion is messy for an authoritarian system and frightening to those who live under it. In the name of discipline and education, yet actually in the service of an economic system which had become our sacred cow, America taught its children to stuff their passions and forget their questions, and thus turn off their minds.

I'm not a conspiracy buff in the traditional sense. The conspiracy that concerns me is our very way of life, our conspiracy of silence about things that matter most. It's an invisible foe because it's the tenor of our collective being. There is no one to oppose because there is no monolithic power source that spews out all the poison of our forgetfulness. We want to forget, after all, because *there are a lot of things we don't even want to know.* Direct confrontation, even if we knew all the ins and outs of America's deepest darkest secrets, is not an option. What we have got to do is rise above, begin thinking again and feeling again like the passionate, authentic, brilliant human beings we were created to be. From that place we will cast a web of insights and manifestation that will disperse malaise and malice, and bring us back to life. The only way to ultimately counter antidemocratic forces is to foster democratic ones.

It's interesting to note some of the differences between Americans and Europeans. The average European is much better educated, much more aware of the true political and social issues that affect his or her daily life, than is the average American. We have become so accustomed to allowing the media to do our thinking for us that we are dangerously ignorant of important matters.

What I've noticed, however, working on both continents, is that as intelligent as Europeans are concerning a particular subject, their enthusiasm for action is not the same as ours. Our political DNA is quite different: they're the children of those who stayed in the Old World, and we're the children of those who came to the New World. Americans are inherently change-agents. There is nothing more *traditionally American* than to *seek to change what we do not like.*

The American propensity to rise up out of oppressive situations and do what we can to transform them sleeps in us, but has not died. And when we awaken, we awaken *big.* You give a group of Americans a thumbnail sketch of an issue that demands our involvement, a 101 overview, and we're jumping up and down on chairs, organizing activity, creating solutions, preparing to act. We leave no doubt that we are indeed the psychological heirs of the men and women who, over two hundred years ago, had what it took to recreate the world. As Thomas Paine proclaimed regarding the American Revolution, "We have it in our power to begin the world over again."

We need a new American Revolution now, a revolution of consciousness and soul.

This begins with our taking responsibility for the abdication of our citizen authority, particularly its moral and spiritual dimensions. We abdicate our power every time we allow ourselves to surrender to the myriad forms of mind-death that pass for culture in America today. If we want a healing in this country, then we will have to take our minds back.

If enough Americans would say, *I will no longer watch too much TV;* if enough Americans would say, *I will read the books I know I should read;* if enough Americans would say, *I will seek my spiritual nature;* if enough Americans would say, *I will vote in every election;* if enough Americans would say, *I will do the things that I know in my heart I should do, and make a passionate stand for the changes that I feel are important*—then America would transform. We've forgotten our identities as the source and protector of power in America, and as a consequence that power is seeping like blood from our wounds.

OUR Founders, by signing the Declaration of Independence, were committing treason against the king of England. If they had failed and were convicted, their punishment would have been the most horrendous death possible. Yet most of us do not show anywhere near their courage or conviction. Rather, our thinking marches right in line with whatever commands the invisible beast hands down. Our biggest fear is the disapproval of his minions.

But there is a secret that every mystical revolutionary should know: The beast has no power whatsoever against the divinely illumined mind. In our hearts and minds lies the power of nonviolence, and that is the power of God alive within us. When harnessed for the collective good, *there is no power in the universe that can stand before its might.*

Know that, and revolution becomes an effortless accomplishment. The heart-filled mind knows no defeat.

But without the strength of an enlivened mind, we become passive observers to our own lives, easy to sell to and easy to control. Thus, the onset of our national disease: citizen anemia. The American people have been spiritually weakened. We know more about fashion at the Oscars than we know about issues that vitally affect our daily lives.

Why should we be aware that Gwynneth Paltrow broke up with Ben Affleck, but not be aware that despite our bounty, America stands almost alone among industrial nations in not providing free basic health care for all, and that 40 million Americans have no access to health care at all? Why should we be aware that Monica Lewinsky wore thong underwear, but not be aware that hunger lines in the United States are growing many millions of people longer every year? Why should we be aware of every model, actor, or celebrity who entered rehab over the last five years, but not be aware that thirteen American children die from gun violence every day? One is reminded of George Washington's comment that "Americans have almost amused themselves out of their liberties." American popular culture is starting to look like an exercise in assisted suicide.

American democracy carries with it extraordinary rights to express ourselves. It is not a political repression of our voices but a psychological and emotional invalidation of our opinions that poses the greatest threat to universal participation in our democracy today. Some of the people with the greatest gifts to give at this time would feel the most insecure about trying to do so. One of the brightest, most technologically capable and materially gifted citizenries in the world is full of people going around thinking, "Who am I to have an opinion? Who am I to make a difference? Who am I to change the world?"

That's when you know they've got you.

America, in fact, has no dearth of genius. What we could do if we wanted to, is nothing short of miraculous. If we applied a fraction of the energy we now use to increase the perceived value of consumer products, to the amelioration of human suffering, we would be a different country and a different world. What we lack is an evolved sense of collective purpose for our talent and intelligence. Our awesome creativity is applied to mainly unimportant ends.

Each of us has within us depths of intelligence and creativity that come forth only in response to meaningful purpose. Many millions of Americans sincerely want to see this country change for the better, and would be more than willing to participate in the effort if they knew how. But it feels as though there is no unified social force field for the effort, no number to call, no place to sign up. People are naturally attracted to a sense of higher, common need; just watch any of us when there is a storm coming through town or a fire down the street. But in America today, service to others is not a social fundamental.

It is, however, a *human* fundamental; it is natural to us, at the deepest level of our being, to love each other. There shouldn't have to be a disaster to bring us together or to inspire us to serve a higher good. Disasters give us social permission to be who we already are. The ancient Greeks used the word *politics* to mean the involvement of the citizen beyond his or her own self, or even family identity, to the larger community of the nation. Politics should not be a place where we merely compete or even negotiate for who gets what, but rather a place where we creatively work together toward a greater good for all.

Service shouldn't be something we do separate from our daily lives; it should become a *way of life*. That, at bottom, is what citizenship is. "Ask not what your country can do for you; ask what you can do for your country" is something that Americans carry in our hearts, much more than we do the promise of a balanced budget. What we most need, as Americans, is to remember—and then act on the memory—that we were born for something far more important than the attainment of mere self-centered goals. We want to feel we're part of something bigger than ourselves. Otherwise, no matter what we do or what we achieve, some little voice at the back of our minds will always say, "Is this all there is?"

AMERICANS are constantly bombarded with the message that things are going so well in America: we're breathing cleaner air and drinking cleaner water, crime is in a free fall and near a twenty-two-year low, and the U.S. economy keeps humming along beautifully. It's like a mantra today that "the economy is good." Skeptics are psychoanalyzed for any inability to take yes for an answer, and all you have to do is spend enough time in trendy stores or restaurants of any American city to see that things are very good.

But there is a dark side to all this, as well. That "good economy" applies to the top 80 per cent of all American wage earners, which is good indeed—*except*. Twenty percent of our citizens—a permanent "underclass"—are completely left out of that economic upswing, a fact routinely swept under the rug by those seeking credit for what's going right.

Behind official statistics lie some very sobering facts. Former Labor Secretary Robert Reich, who served in President Clinton's first term, has said, "There are still millions of people desperately trying to stay afloat.... But Americans are segregated by income as never before, so it is far easier to pretend the worse off don't exist. They're out of sight."

Like Germany in the early thirties, Rome before it fell, and

France before the Revolution, the United States is a nation in denial. We routinely dance while those on the other side of town are bleeding. We are not a selfish people; I think the average American isn't even aware of the huge amount of unnecessary human suffering that still exists in this country. There are those who would have us *not* see. I am always amazed at politicians on both sides of the aisle who constantly drone on about "middle-class values," "middle-class" this or "middle-class" that. What are "lower-class" values or "upper-class" values, for that matter? Do lower-class people love God or their children any less? What happened to our Founders' vision of a classless society? Why should a political and media elite be able to make 36 million poverty-stricken people seem invisible?

The plight of the poor in America today and the desperate conditions of life in our inner cities are a tinderbox just waiting for a match. Our political leaders, many of whom are aware that the tinderbox exists, seem to think that they won't be reelected if they mention it. They spend more time and money investigating one another than addressing the critical social and economic injustices that rage among us and threaten our children.

Many of those leaders would say that this is irresponsible, incendiary talk; our children will *not* be threatened by all this injustice and suffering, because our fine responsible civil servants are working day and night to make sure we build enough prisons, fast enough, to lock up anyone who has even the slightest urge to act out their desperation. Prison building is the single largest urban industry in America, prisons are half of all public housing built in this country in the last ten years, and we already have a greater portion of our citizens behind bars than any other nation in the world. We could call this our "Bastille policy."

We are saying to people who are as afraid of the police as they are of the criminals, whose children do not have safe schools, whose children are at risk even walking to school, whose children do not even have enough school supplies and textbooks at their schools, whose children have practically no chance of finding a job in the neighborhood even if they do by some miracle muster the courage and the inner strength to make it through that dangerous maze and graduate from high school, that you'd better fly right now and not make a single false step from here on out, *because we've had it up to here with helping you.*

In an interview for the *New York Times* in April 1997, former President Jimmy Carter said,

> The Government has changed dramatically since I was in the White House. I was with Presidents Bush and Ford early last week and we all agreed that since all of us left office, there has been a hardening of concern in the Federal Government and the other levels of government, a sternness about people who are unfortunate, a condemnation of people who are different from ourselves, a discrimination against people who are poor and deprived that is quite traumatic in its impact.

In his very fine book *Dialogues,* Oakland Mayor and former California Governor Jerry Brown interviews author Jonathan Kozol about conditions in New York City's neighborhood of Mott Haven. Mott Haven is one of the poorest neighborhoods of the South Bronx, which is the poorest Congressional district in the country. Ninety-five percent of the children live in poverty. Roughly two-thirds of these children are Puerto Rican, and one-third African American. The New York City jail on Riker's Island, now the largest penal colony in the world, is just a short distance away, and houses 20,000 people on any given day. The prison is almost entirely filled with people of color, many of them the parents, uncles, aunts, and grandparents of the children of Mott Haven. It is estimated that a quarter of all young mothers in the neighborhood are HIV positive. Doctors Without Borders, a French group that routinely helps people in the Third World, has come in to help the South Bronx. People in other countries are often more aware than we are of the most dire situations in our midst.

Eighteen minutes away by subway is the Upper East Side of New York City. The richest among us often live so close to the poorest among us, and yet we live a world apart. If you're walking down Madison Avenue on a beautiful sunny day, the neighborhood of Mott Haven is likely to be the last thing on your mind. If you've read the *New York Times* this morning, in fact, you might have seen reference to the fact that things are going so well in New York.

Lovers of democracy might well question why a small child growing up in the South Bronx, who is every bit as much an American citizen as is a corporate CEO living on Park Avenue, should receive *less* help from the government! In one of the better-known stories displaying the irony of our current situation, Lawrence Bossidy, CEO of Allied Signal Corporation, complained about "hundreds of thousands of able-bodied people who stay on welfare for years at a time"—but his company is one of our largest recipients of corporate welfare. According to *Time* magazine (November 16, 1998), over the past five years Allied tripled its profits to $1.2 billion (with earnings that total $4 billion), but received more than $150 million in state and federal corporate subsidies, loans and guarantees overseas, breaks on real estate taxes, federal research contracts, and incentives to build new offices. These words of Dr. King still echo: "When they give it to rich people, they call it a subsidy. When they give it to poor people, they call it a hand-out."

To those doing well, it seems that times are so great in America. But what we're experiencing is merely a sunset effect, where the sun looks so glorious just before it goes down to inevitably darkening skies. The economic forecast might be cheery and great, but an economic forecast is not the same as a moral forecast. What we do to the least of these, we do to Him. Economic forecasts can lie, and the media can lie. But history does not lie. And neither does the heart. There is a moral vision at the center of all things.

Morality is a light with many facets.

Social conservatives tend to concentrate mainly on private morality, whereas social liberals focus more on public morality. To conservatives, someone's having an adulterous affair might be viewed as a serious violation of moral law. To a liberal, the American government's abandonment of the health and education of millions of disadvantaged children in favor of tax breaks for our wealthiest citizens is an egregious violation of moral law.

A spiritual discussion is not the same as a moral discussion. Moral principles, while not relative in themselves, can be interpreted in many ways. Spiritual principles, on the other hand, are based on objective, discernable laws of consciousness.

The spiritual conversation does not *take sides.* It merely states the deeper issue, favoring only the enlightenment of the human race. It is a set of principles on which the universe is ordered. Spiritual law is not personal but impersonal, like physical laws. If Hitler strode into the sunlight, then Hitler got sun. If Mother Teresa had walked off a platform, then Mother Teresa would have fallen down. No one gets different treatment by physical laws—*or* spiritual laws—depending on whether they're "nice" or not.

The cornerstone of spiritual law is the law of cause and effect, or what in the Eastern traditions is called *karma.* As we know from physics, every action has a reaction. That principle, applied to even the tiniest thought, is the essence of spirituality. It is the basis for the Golden Rule, which is at the heart of all religious teaching: Do unto others as you would have others do unto you, *because they will.* Or if they don't, *someone else will.* In a way, that's all you need to know.

It's not just that God said we should love one another. He also created the universe in such a way that, in time, we are sure to learn to do just that. If everything we do has a consequence, if everything we do comes back to us, then surely we will come in time to learn that it is ultimately in our own best interests to put out only what we would want to get back.

How this applies to politics is interesting. Millions, probably billions of people on earth are aware that the law of cause and effect is simply the way things are. But what we have not yet deeply considered—certainly not in the United States—is that this principle holds for collective actions in the same way it holds for individual actions.

If Steve violates the law of love, then Steve is going to have to pay the cosmic price. If Steve's government violates the law of love, then Steve's nation will have to pay the cosmic price. And since Steve lives there, *his life will be affected.* Steve, at that time, will not be able to appeal to some higher court saying, "But God, I didn't know what my government was doing!" Particularly not in a society when Steve *would* have known had Steve been look-ing, and Steve *would* have realized had Steve been thinking, and Steve *could* have made a difference had Steve exercised his power to do so.

I once heard Walter Cronkite give a speech in which he said that when Allied forces liberated the Nazi concentration camps, Germans who lived within miles of the camps rushed to meet Allied soldiers saying, "We didn't know! We didn't know what was happening there!" But, said Cronkite, they were still respon-sible—for they had tolerated the shutting down of a free press in Germany, and once that has occurred, then *anything* can happen.

In many ways, we are accountable not only for what we know but also for what we *should* have known.

As long as we're on the subject of Hitler, by the way, it's a good time in our history to remember that he was *democratically elected.*

Another plea with the universe that doesn't always work well is, "My boss made me do it," or, "It was someone else's decision." Nazi war criminals were sent to their deaths by the Nuremburg tribunal, which held, like Thoreau, that conscience is a higher law than government. If your government is perpetrating something that violates the higher law of life as you understand it, then theoretically it is your responsibility to say so and your responsiblity to refuse to participate. *Satyagraha* was Gandhi's term for the refusal to participate in unjust systems, and he posited that, over time, the moral authority of such refusal turns into political force.

When it comes to the behavior of national governments and huge multinational conglomerates, it is very easy for the individual to look away. It is very easy to say, "This has nothing to do with me. I can't make a difference anyway." But from a metaphysical perspective, it behooves us to remember that the universe *never looks away.* It registers everything, even to the last detail, and what boomerangs back at your nation, boomerangs back at you whether you have been looking or not.

Another principle is the illusion of time. In an individual's life, it is fairly easy to see that if I am unfair to Dorothy, then Dorothy will probably do something to react to that quite soon. In a small enough context, it is easy to see how karma works. But the size of the context means nothing to the universe. In a nation's life, particularly one as mighty as our own, military and economic power can bolster the illusion that the cosmic order can somehow be modified—*but it cannot.* We figure we won't be punished for transgressions against some small nation in the

Third World because our military might is so extraordinary, who would dare retaliate? But whether or not that nation can retaliate is irrelevant. Nature retaliates. All that is relevant is the law of the universe; what we do *will* come back to us, and—consider this—*if not to us today, then to our children tomorrow.*

It is our thoughts that determine the forces set in motion by the universe. If our thoughts are loving, then love will return to us. If our thoughts are not loving, if our national power rests more on "brute force" than on "soul force," then fear is what will return to us.

If our response to nuclear proliferation is merely to negotiate the eradication of nuclear weapons, let's say, but we have not healed our thoughts of attack, then attack will simply return to us in another form—such as chemical or germ warfare. The deepest problem is not nuclear bombs, but rather the attitudes they reflect. *Only when our thoughts are healed will the planet be safe for ourselves and our children.*

President Franklin Roosevelt wrote these words in 1945, for a Jefferson Day address that he died before being able to deliver: "More than an end to war, we want an end to the beginnings of all wars."

Those beginnings are inside us.

At the beginning of the twentieth century, Westerners were somewhat naively hopeful that science and technology could solve all the problems of humanity. Now, almost one hundred years later, how painful and poignant is the realization that this is anything but true. The forces of humanly manufactured powers merely follow our command. They can be instruments of hate or instruments of love, instruments of war or instruments of peace, depending on how our minds direct them. But no thoughts are neutral; all minds create at some level. Energy is never static. At this point in history, something either leads to a better world or else leads to one more dangerous. What does not create, on some level, destroys. Every thought is based on either love or fear, and then extends accordingly. *We are free to choose what we want to think, but we are not free to escape the forces set in motion by the mental choices we make.*

The task before the human race is to become a human family. Nothing less will ensure our safety, or even guarantee the survival of our species, at a time when the world has become so small and the stakes have become so high.

The question is, do we, the current generation, have what it takes to live up to the critical challenges of the time in which we live? Are we made of the "right stuff," psychologically, morally, and in every other way, to stave off the dangers and fortify the security of the civilized world?

Certain generations of Americans have jumped up and down to say, "We do! We do!" Ours doesn't seem to have decided yet. . . .

THERE are interesting psychological differences between the generation of Americans that fought World War II, and their children. That earlier generation surrendered five years of their lives to wage the war. After that, they wanted little more than to lie back on the couch, put their feet up on the coffee table, and drink another beer. Their psychological slogan was, "Don't talk to me about what I should do for anyone else. I did my bit." Seen from today's perspective, who can blame them? It could be argued, in current jargon, that that was an entire generation undergoing posttraumatic stress! Can our generation even imagine what it would mean to take on the Nazis for five years, and then never even go to therapy to discuss it?

General Eisenhower was the Supreme Allied Commander during World War II, and then President of the United States from 1952 until 1960. He was clearly not of the intellectual stature of his opponent in both Presidential races, Adlai Stevenson. Some have even suggested that the message of his election was, in effect, "Give me Eisenhower—I don't want to have to think too much." But certainly there was more to Eisenhower's popularity than that. Americans were led brilliantly by Eisenhower during the war, and would have understandably felt comfortable with the thought of letting him lead the nation after that. I also think that Eisenhower himself, with his unique vantage point for viewing the devastating effect of World War II on the generation that fought it, would have had a natural tendency to want to comfort people in the following years, to let them rest from too much strain, to at least unconsciously protect us from any further, critical public challenges.

That generation had *earned* a vacation from too much civic strain, and someone like Adlai Stevenson—by sheer virtue of the fact that he himself thought so deeply—could not avoid challenging others to do the same, pointing people's attention to things that were not very much fun or easy to look at. "I just fought a war, damn it. Now I have to think about things that are wrong here at home?" The next thought could very naturally be, "AND WHEN DO I GET MINE?"

"Nope," the nation said. "I want a vacation. I want some money. I want a pool. I want *the Fifties.*"

And then, of course, the baby boom. Millions of us were thus brought up by mentally vacationing parents, and simply because we lived in the house with them, we went on vacation, too! The difference between our generation and theirs, though, is that they had earned their vacation—and we did not. They had collectively given of themselves to make the world a better place, which awarded them a badge of honor they well deserve. We've never had that experience.

War initiated that generation into bravery. Our generation has still not completed its initiation, its rite of passage into a most truly serious, responsible adulthood. Vietnam was an unjust war, and it speaks well of us, not ill, that we rejected it on moral grounds. History challenged an earlier generation to wage war, and it challenges our generation to wage peace. We began to do that, and then we stopped. Now we are middle-aged people still in search of something to cut our teeth on. Every generation has its lessons, but not every generation learns them.

Had the sixties not happened, I think the baby-boomer generation would have made its mark in the most glorious way. We had the leaders to lead us through the door marked "Glory," but when they died, we felt the door shut in our faces. What actually happened bears a closer look. Like Moses leading the Israelites to the Promised Land but not being able to enter it himself, the Kennedys and King took us up to the door but they themselves could not walk through.

Opening that door is *our* job.

For the last thirty years, my generation has just been milling about outside the door—doing a lot and yet, in terms of furthering the spiritual evolution of the human race, actually doing very little. We've mastered the art of "making things better for me," but have given astoundingly little attention to "making things better for us."

Millions remember that we once saw the door marked "A Better World for Everyone"; now almost all of us have lost the sense that we will open it in our lifetime. The idealists of yesterday have become the cynics of today. Yet this moment presents an opportunity for change. The baby boomers have reached menopause, when nature says, "We don't need you for our physical purposes anymore. You can die now, if you want to." Exactly. Our ovaries and sperm are no longer needed to propagate the species. We will slowly begin to die now, unless we will choose to be reborn.

Rebirth, for all of America, means resurrecting the characterological audacity to start new things, which is at the heart of the American spirit. To reinvent, to recreate, to say "No, we can do better"—these are the forces that gave us birth and would redeem us now. New possibilities for life on earth are waiting to be born.

In this emerging new cycle of our national life, it behooves us to remember we are the *United* States, not the disunited states. At this point in the life of our country, and the life of the world, we will remember we're together, or we will surely die apart. That joining, and the sense of community it engenders, is the cornerstone of the new America.

With the new millennium, there is a yearning among us to apply our talents to collective ends. Millions go home at night, to nice apartments, nice houses, nice furniture, nice electronic equipment, even nice bodies beside them, and yet deep in their hearts say, "God, I'm bored." We long for a more genuinely passionate life, and for a deeper purpose to living it. We want to throw off the invisible chains of a wealthy slave condition, in which our genius has been co-opted to serve no higher god than mammon, which is no god at all. We're grateful for where we've been, but we want to start a new cycle now. The current America just recycles the old; the new America is truly new.

As long as we are living, we have the greatest God-given power: the power to choose again. Many signs—from CEOs of oil companies beginning to speak of the importance of environmental consciousness, to greater local citizen activism occurring throughout the United States, to, most important of all, the intense activation of spiritual consciousness here and throughout the world—make clear that a time of awakening is truly at hand. We are ready to wake up from a very, very long nap. We are ready to get back to the Great Work of being alive.

Author Barbara Marx Hubbard has said that the greatest poverty of our times is the poverty of those who are not giving their spiritual gifts. "Twenty percent live at base level need, and eighty percent at spiritual need. And if the 80 percent were giving their gifts, the 20 percent wouldn't be in material poverty."

Like a new mother who feels physical pressure to give her milk, we too feel internal pressure to give of what we have to the generations coming after us. Nothing short of that is deep enough to satisfy our need. We want to be *more* than contenders; we want to be contributors to something bigger than ourselves.

Just as there is a so-called art of waging war, so there is an art of waging peace. "True peace," said Dr. King, "is not merely the absence of some negative force—tension, confusion, or war; it is the presence of some positive force—justice, good will and brotherhood."

We need to *declare* peace now, with as much serious effort and intention as that with which a nation declares war. Fear-based thinking is essentially a war mentality, and who among us does not live with fear. Our efforts to be spiritually healed, to find the love that sets us free, is our effort to become not only more peaceful ourselves but also instruments of peace in a war-torn world. Gandhi said, "We must *be* the change we want to see happen in the world."

Until a critical mass of Americans commits to the establishment of a nonviolent society, violence will continue to plague us. The issue, ultimately, isn't whether gun manufacturers or the producers of violent media and video games are more responsible for violence among our children, in Colorado or anywhere else. The most important issue is to recognize that both gun manufacturers and violent video manufacturers serve the same false god, and his color is green. Blood money is hardly true prosperity. And as long as short-term economic interests are society's bottom line, then our children will be underserved. Caring for our children does not always serve society's short term economic interest, but it does serve our long-term humanitarian one. We cannot have it both ways, and our pretending otherwise is threatening to destroy us. Ultimately, only a massive change of heart will change our societal direction in any serious way.

Love is more than a feeling; it is a choice, a commitment, a stand we take, or it is nothing. A stand for heart is the essence of the new, nonviolent revolution now brewing in America. We are looking within, where we are finding our true power. And we are committed to expressing our power in meaningful, effective ways.

It is time for us to repudiate America's culture of violence, not just by blaming others but by inventorying our own hearts. Some of us need to surrender our guns, some of us need to surrender our violent books and videos, and some of us need to surrender the unforgiveness we harbor and have harbored in our hearts for years.

Until we, the American people, fundamentally change, nothing is going to be fundamentally different. Our children will continue to kill and be killed. Our use of antidepressant drugs will continue to soar. Our water and food will essentially become poisoned. And our very freedom will become mere memory.

The American experiment, in that awful yet no longer impossible scenario, will have failed.

Unless we choose otherwise, of course . . . and while there is still time.

THE fabric of American society can only be rewoven one stitch at a time: one person forgiven, one child read to, one sick person prayed for, one elder given respect and made to feel needed, one prisoner rehabilitated, one mourner given comfort. These actions, when performed sincerely, emanate from spiritual ground that is itself the healing of our problems, as our separation from that ground of being has itself been our primary wound. Like the mythical lost continent of Atlantis, there is a ground now submerged beneath the subconscious waters, visible in ancient times perhaps but not visible now, set to rise again, to reappear. Our initial tenderness, wonderment, and innocence have been suppressed and marginalized by the world we have built—the world of modern "progress." It is only when we fall in love, marry, give birth, grieve openly, or prepare to die that we dare to show our real face, to shine the light that glows within us. Our failure to be more authentically human is threatening to destroy the world.

In a country where our political right to live creatively is so awesomely assured, there is yet within most of us the feeling that a beautiful instrument is in some way going unplayed. There is a saying in the Jewish prayer book, "Sad is he who does not sing, and when he dies his music dies with him." Something goes unsung in most Americans today, though there is yet within each of us the urging of an internal conductor, exhorting and preparing us to sing.

While earthly resources are finite, spiritual ones are not. In all of us there is divine potential and the natural propensity to reach for it. In a nation of 266 million people, there is a stunning collection of unmined spiritual gold. As we each mature into a deeper understanding of our lives and why we're living them, that understanding itself becomes the womb of a new America. As each of us awakens to the preciousness of our individual right to make a difference in this world—and the cosmic momentum that will support us when we try—we become a powerful wave of resistence to the forces of fear. It is not just our capacity to say no to what we don't want that is our power to renew the world around us. It is our deeper power to say yes to our own creative abilities and yes to the light within others, which is the healing balm for the American soul. Each generation brings forth new life, physically and spiritually, or life will have to stop. Each of us might ask ourselves now, "Am I ready to bring forth new life, for myself, for my nation, for my world?"

When enough of us start asking deeper questions, then answers will miraculously appear. Serbia forces us into deeper questioning. Columbine High School forces us into deeper questioning. The difficulty and heartbreak of these questions are forcing us to our knees.

And that is exactly where we need to be.

5

THE ETERNALS
OF FINANCE

I N the Middle Ages, people believed that their lives were affected by "good spirits" and "bad spirits." With the advent of the Renaissance and then the scientific revolution, people gave up such folly. Heh, heh, heh, heh, heh, heh.

History, whether personal or worldly, unfolds according to a universal rhythm: thesis meets antithesis, creating new synthesis. Everything in life impels its own opposition, and the opposing forces then birth something new.

Yes, Renaissance thinking freed the Western mind from the overmystification of the Middle Ages. But no, the scientific revolution was not the truth, the whole truth, and nothing but the truth. Yes, there are objective, discernable laws of the physical universe, but yes, there are also mysterious, unexplainable phenomena that mechanistic thinking cannot grasp. The cutting edges of science now support certain ancient spiritual traditions.

Which takes us back to "good spirits" and "bad spirits." No, we're not in the Middle Ages anymore, but neither did "bad spirits" go away just because we stopped believing in them. "Bad spirits" are fear-based thought forms, and they are not merely personal. They are collective, as well. In fact, because on a spiritual level all minds are joined, all thought-forms are on some level collective. As we have discussed before, mere external remedy does not ultimately solve a problem, unless the root thinking that produced the problem is transformed within the mind. As long as anyone still holds a racist thought, slavery isn't really over. As long as anyone still feels that one group of people is "better" than any other, then war will not be over. As long as anyone thinks that someone else's being empowered disempowers *them*, then injustice will not disappear from the earth.

For instance, historians now believe that during the Middle Ages, somewhere between 800,000 and 9 million people were burned at the stake, 85 percent of whom were women. While we no longer burn witches, we have still not completely routed out of the Western mind the suspicion that there is something dangerous about female power. On a psychic level, powerful women are still burning. We've merely changed the consonant from "w" to "b."

Fear-based archetypes live beyond time or place. They inhabit the eternal regions of the subconscious mind. Scientific or social or political progress can temporarily render them ineffective, but cannot rout them out. Thoughts of fear merely mutate when chased, taking different forms in different times and places. Reason cannot exorcise what is essentially a spiritual darkness. Fear grows like an uncontrollable fungus on the soulless layers of the modern mind, leaving us with an insatiable appetite for a stew of externals that cannot feed us. Traditional therapy cannot begin to touch the spiritual malaise of the times in which we live. It is a spiritual, not a psychological disease, that threatens to destroy us. In the words of Carl Jung, "Only spirit can cure spirit."

Our disease is not that fifty thousand people on earth are dying of hunger each day, while there is no dearth of food on the planet; our disease is that we are willing to tolerate it. Our disease is not that millions of American children are living lives of hardship and despair as deep as that of any Third World country, while politicians of both parties appear on political talk shows every night and don't feel the need to mention it; our disease is that they can get away with this. Our disease is not that while the United States is the richest nation in the world, we give away only six-tenths of 1 percent in aid to nations less fortunate than we; our disease is that any politician suggesting we be more charitable would probably lose his or her next election!

Only a spiritual awakening can heal us. Our national conscience is impacted now, held as in a cave, waiting for resurrection and release. "Bad spirits" are floating around us, old, old archetypes that appear and reappear throughout human history, mocking and destroying the most evolved human dreams.

Take the guise of the Inquisitor. He had a heyday in the Middle Ages, as mentioned before, burning hundreds of thousands of people at the stake, particularly women. He detests, among other things, anything sexual. Sex scares him because he is an antilife force, and sex is both life affirming and life creating. The archetype made an appearance quite recently in the impeachment of President Clinton, but the thinking of the American people was fairly alert to the disguised marauding of our rights to sexual privacy. In Europe, where the Inquisition actually occurred, people learned long ago that the Inquisitor is much more dangerous than sex. Americans recently stared down the Inquisitor in our midst, but we did not defeat him. Only God can do that. The Inquisitor is not dead but merely sleeping. The archetype will be vanquished only when it is finally transformed, seen completely for what it is, forgiven and then surrendered to the forces of divine correction.

Telling Kenneth Starr to go away doesn't ultimately kill the Inquisitor. He doesn't live in Kenneth Starr to begin with; he only used him. He lives in all of us. Behind Kenneth Starr there is another Kenneth Starr, just as behind Bill Clinton, there is another Bill Clinton, and behind Saddam Hussein there is another Saddam Hussein. "Spirits" inhabit bodies. As Lincoln said, it is the "angels of our better natures" that we must choose to allow to direct our lives—and there are the good and the bad, the loving and the fearful, in all of us.

In fact, what we attack in others we merely fortify in ourselves. That is because, at the deepest level, we *are* each other. That is the mystical meaning of the "one begotten son."

So what are we to do when we see the "bad spirits" taking shape in our world?

First, we begin with the power of awareness. There is a way to look at the tactics of the Inquisitional mentality without hating the Inquisitor. *Agape* love is brotherly love, in which we reject the deeds of the oppressor without rejecting the oppressor himself. What you hate, you can't get rid of. The warden is as imprisoned as the prisoner.

Second, we must commit not to participate with injustice—even if it is turned into law, by the way, and even though there is usually some candy thrown our way if we *do* participate.

Third, we must ask God to remove the inquisitor from *within us,* for we live in a holographic universe, and if it's out there, then it's in here, and if it's in here, then it's out there.

Fourth, it behooves us to pray for the Inquisitor outside us—whoever he or she is—for as we know, the Inquisitor is merely showing us to ourselves.

THE world has heard plenty about the "democratic spirit." It's a cliché, but it's also a very real thing. It is a force of consciousness, a love of liberty and an embrace of the notion that there is a brilliant goodness in all of us that deserves to come forth, and creates a veritable garden of the world when it does.

And what about an "antidemocratic" spirit? Does that exist, too? Absolutely, it does. It was born as fear's response to the equality of souls, which was the original "democracy." Democratic thought and democratic revolutions are expressions of our divine drive back toward the freedom condition, which is our natural birthright as children of God. "Antidemocracy" takes many forms, but they are always marked by brute force and domination of one group of people by another.

The "antidemocracy" spirit takes form in the world as some variation of aristocracy. In Europe's *ancien régime,* the aristocracy was quite aboveboard about who and what it was. Today, one of the most virulent antidemocracy, aristocratic forces does not announce itself as such, or even necessarily see itself that way. It is money itself that now threatens to dominate the peoples of the world, even the so-called free governments of the world.

In 1998, fifty-one of the world's one hundred largest economies were not nations, but transnational corporations. Today, these corporations are literally more powerful than governments. An ugly behind-the-scenes drama, to which the United States is not immune, is that of free, sovereign nations succumbing to what is in effect the power of a corporate colonialization process. The world's most powerful economic institutions push treaties by which nations and communities are *prohibited* from passing laws that would weaken the hold of global capitalism in that country. Nation after nation is going down, lured by the illusion of economic security sold to unsuspecting citizens. We are giving in to a corporate dominance that would culturally homogenize the world, suppress the vast majority of its citizens, and run rampant over our natural resources. International financial institutions carry a mandate backed by the power of the strongest nations in the world, particularly the United States: eliminate all barriers to the free international movement of goods and capital, ensuring the right to such movement even against the intrusion of democratic governments and the people to which they are accountable. This effectively makes a mockery of democracy. Can you imagine a treaty that says to a nation that it cannot pass this or that law if it makes it harder for a large corporation to make money in that country? That is exactly what the General Agreement on Tariffs and Trade (GATT) does. What difference does it make who our leaders are, or how much they put the good of their citizens before the good of transnational corporate entities, if those entities have become more powerful than governments?

IN America today, free-market capitalism cannot legitimately claim that, where more money is produced for a corporate entity, life by definition is made better for everyone. If the cost of doing business is ecological distress that threatens the welfare of people and planet, if American workers continue to lose social and economic ground in the unraveling of the social contract between management and labor, if executive compensation packages continue to eat the lion's share of this country's profits, if money continues to rule Washington and turn the American government into little more than a slave to the market, then democracy will be sacrificed. Our almost tragic deference to the needs of the free-market capitalist economy goes even against the philosophy of Adam Smith, who proclaimed that the free market cannot exist outside an ethical context. Part of what makes capitalism such a good economic system is that it allows people freedom. What freedom means, however, is that each of us has even more responsibility to ask ourselves, "Does what I am about to do serve merely a short-term economic good or a long-term social good, as well?"

If we decide that improving the life of the average American is more important than consolidating more power in the hands of a corporate elite, then we had better go back into politics, with all our intelligence and all our heart. And do not expect either Democrats or Republicans to tell it like it is regarding the corporate colonialism running rampant over this planet. In the absence of campaign finance reform, both major political parties are beholden to corporate money.

One of the things that has impacted me most over the last few years is how many elected officials, when they hear complaints about the kinds of things I am discussing here, can only say, "I know, I know," with the same fear and frustration as so many of us feel. It makes you wonder who's really running the country, when the people holding all that so-called power are feeling as disempowered as the rest of us.

Our hope lies in a nonviolent revolution coming up from the streets, centered in local politics, growing in various communities, open to new ideas and third-party candidates, calling on all the powers of the soul, pressing forward despite the spin and veritable shadow dance of current corporate influence, not only over so much of what we do but over even what we think.

CORPORATE interests—not the people of the United States—for all intents and purposes now own America.

Moneyed interests control the political process, routinely pouring so many millions of dollars into so many political campaigns as to have completely corrupted the process. This is not a secret anymore. The health and well-being of corporate structures are placed before the health and well-being of individuals and communities, no matter how many people are trapped in poverty by the process; no matter how much the preferred corporate policies widen the already alarming gap between rich and poor; no matter how much human havoc is wreaked among working people whose livelihoods are threatened by corporate restructuring and downsizing; no matter how many more known carcinogens are poured into our ground, our air, and our food; and no matter how many young people are sent to decrepit schools that cannot even afford textbooks, where teaching becomes by definition more crowd control than education, in communities where real chances for young people making it in the world get smaller and smaller every day.

The top 5 percent of our population takes home half the nation's income; huge and profitable companies lay off thousands of employees for no other reason than to increase their short-term stock prices and their already outrageous executive compensation packages. Congress grants huge subsidies and tax breaks amounting to billions of dollars in "corporate welfare"—and the life and safety of the average American are increasingly crushed underneath it all.

Gargantuan economic concerns, whose financial interests are unabashedly placed ahead of the collective good, pour through the halls of our government like lava. We do not spend billions upon billions of dollars more to support certain industries than to support our children for any other reason than that organized business interests can afford highly paid lobbyists to make it happen, in both legal and illegal ways. The influence of money on the political process is a fast-growing cancer in America. It grows in small ways and big ways, every day of the year.

CORPORATIONS of themselves are not the problem, but only their undue and at times unethical influence. We don't want to turn *off* the system. There is nothing beautiful about what happens in a society when money stops circulating. Our challenge is not to destroy capitalism but to transform its dominant ethos; not to childishly and blindly demonize the corporation but to make a case for the importance—and ultimate benefit to all—of conscience within it.

If you bought this book, I will receive money. Capitalism has been good to me, and I know a bit about its upside. I celebrate my economic freedom as much as anyone. But there is no amount of money I can make that will protect my child from the explosion of horror that will occur in this country if we do not commit to a serious effort at universal access to the opportunities that capitalism affords.

As a child I was fed, stimulated culturally, safe in my environment, and cared for medically. I was told I was valuable by the world around me—psychologically as well as materially, I had a reasonable *chance* of success. And it was not just my parents, or our religious community, that gave me those things. There was a larger culture of which I was a part, believing in me and supporting me in myriad ways both large and small: in short, I was set up to succeed. But millions of American children today are absolutely set up to fail. It's one thing to say that everyone has to climb the ladder of success by him or herself; it's another thing entirely to make the bottom rung too high for a child to reach, and then condemn him when he can't climb from there! That is what is happening to millions of children in America, each and every day.

Children cannot provide their own health care; children cannot be responsible for their own education; children cannot create their own cultural stimulation before someone teaches them how. To provide those things to all of America's children is our responsibility as a society dedicated to self-governance. What we are doing today, as evidenced by so many undereducated, under-cared-for, throw-away children, is abdicating our moral responsibility to the development of millions of American lives, and then acting horrified when they turn to dysfunctional behavior.

We need to do more than rally to serve all America's underprivileged citizens; we need to ask ourselves what is wrong in our society—including our public policies—that there are so many people living in desperate conditions to begin with.

In the 1830s, President Andrew Jackson sought to break the financial chokehold that he thought the Bank of the U.S. had over American life. His words make sense today:

> It is to be regretted that the rich and the powerful too often bend the acts of government to their selfish purposes. Distinctions in society will always exist ... but when the law undertakes to add to these natural and just advantages artificial distinctions ... exclusive privileges to make the rich richer and the more potent more powerful, the humble members of society ... have a right to complain of the injustice of their Government. There are no necessary evils in government. Its evils exist only in its abuses.

> It is time to pause in our career to review our principles, and if possible revive that devoted patriotism and spirit of compromise which distinguished the sages of the Revolution and the fathers of our Union.... [W]e can at least take a stand against all new grants of monopolies and exclusive privileges, against any prostitution of our Government to the advancement of the few at the expense of the many....

We hear many people say today that poverty is a "charity" issue, and that the government should not be involved in charity. According to that line of thinking, it should be the purview of nonprofits, churches, and so on, to support America's disadvantaged citizens. But as someone who has founded nonprofits, who understands the importance of charity work, and now leads a religious congregation, I know very well that charity cannot compensate for lack of social justice. When I look at the advantages of my own child and the relative disadvantages of children a few miles away, I don't just think that I should be involved in charity work. I think that the child on the other side of town is being denied her *rights* in a democratic society, and I fear for my own grandchildren, years from now, if I and my fellow citizens don't stem the tide of growing injustice in this country.

We have a fire in our house and it's considered not polite to mention it. Pointing out the economic inequities in our midst is viewed as incendiary talk, often labeled as fostering "class warfare." But in reality, class warfare in this country is what is already being waged against the poor among us, and the prevailing system feels it has the upper hand in that war because our prison system is large enough to handle the expressions of rage that inevitably arise among our lower classes.

A friend of mine pointed out to me recently that hungry kids don't learn, and hungry adults can't hold down a job. The hungry among us *exist*. They are not figments of anyone's imagination. What is going on in our psyches that we are conducting our national business as though this elephant in our living room does not exist? We are all too polite to mention it, *when times, after all, are so good*. Some would say to Thomas Jefferson today, "What are *you* complaining about?! *You* have a nice house!!"

What has happened in this country in the last few decades is that economic opportunity has been systematically drawn upwards, and now the smallest portion of our citizens control the majority of our wealth. With economic opportunity moving higher all the time, the middle class becomes crushed: the greatest fear admitted by most Americans today is job insecurity. So what does the power elite say to those now crushed from above? That the problem is those right below you—those who are actually being crushed even more!

There is too much needless suffering our midst, forming a pressure cooker right beneath us. Nothing is more dangerous to social stability than a large population of desperate people, and that is what America has. We already employ more private than public police in this country, so scared are we of "those people" who might stalk us in the night, coming over from the other side of town to do us harm in some way. But who are those people? Were they born to their dysfunctions? Did they look up into their mothers' eyes while babies and say, "I think I want to be a drug dealer when I grow up?" Did their mother have job training available to her, or mass transit, if she was willing to try to better herself? Did the child's father really "abandon" the baby, or did an unequal system of justice just as often throw him into jail for an offense that someone else might have been merely slapped and sent home for, leaving the man to rot in jail and the baby to grow up without him? Who among us would do well with poverty? And who among us will do well in the future, if we continue to ignore this ignobility in our midst?

I was sitting having brunch with a friend at a trendy location in Los Angeles. Cindy Crawford's boyfriend had just walked by.

"It's not enough to just give money to the poor, Marianne," said my friend, sipping his mimosa. "The poor are going to have to change their *attitudes.*"

I asked him who he thought had a better chance at a positive attitude today: the people having brunch in this beautiful restaurant, or people about ten miles away on the other side of town.

Bobby Kennedy used to say that until you have spent one full day in the neighborhood of the inner-city poor in our society, you have no right to condemn them or judge them.

A classic tool of demagoguery is to identify a type of person and then use that example to condemn the entire group the person belongs to. Every group has its shadow face. Yes, there are Jewish slumlords, but that is not who Jews *are.* Yes, there are Islamic terrorists, but that is not who Muslims *are.* Yes, there are judgmental, hateful people who call themselves Christians, but that is not who Christians are. Yes, there are screaming gay hysterics, but that is not who gay people are. Yes, there are violent black men, but that is not who black men are. And yes, there are lazy, unreliable, up-to-no-good, just-wanting-a-handout poor people in America, but *that is not who the poor in America are.*

The poor is who my grandfather was; was yours? The immigrant is who my grandparents were; were yours? The desperate are who I once was; were you?

New paradigm thinking, relevant to all human endeavors, posits the interconnectedness of all people. The poet John Donne wrote, "No man is an island, entire of itself; every man is a piece of the continent, a part of the main." This is not just an economic, social, or emotional truth; it is a *spiritual*, or *ultimate*, truth and thus will always be reflected across the board in human affairs.

No one can win at the expense of another and long retain his or her advantage. If we severely oppress people economically, they will act out their desperation in ways that ultimately endanger all of us. Harsher prison sentences and other tightened screws will hardly set us free.

The average American, for obvious reasons, has not recently driven through the streets of our most devastated communities. With their jobless rates three to four times the national average, the millions of residents of America's urban wastelands are caught in a culture of vicious poverty as deep as that of a Third World country.

So many millions of dollars have been spent on public relations to convince America that things are basically okay, except for the suffering of a few lazy drug fiends and their liberal friends, that millions of Americans have been duped into believing that the victims are the bad guys and that those who disdain America's first principles are the saviors of our disintegrating culture.

When someone in America now says "the economy is good,"

---

we should ask ourselves, "Good for whom?" The inner-city poor in America have lived for nearly thirty years with social and economic conditions as bad as those endured during the worst days of the Depression. The Depression lasted for ten years maximum, and was considered a national catastrophe. It would have been inconceivable for Americans, or the American government at that time, not to try to alleviate the suffering of those whose lives were wrecked by the Great Depression. President Roosevelt created jobs through the Public Works Administration and the Works Progress Administration. President Eisenhower would later help rebuild the economy of the rural South through the Economic Development Administration, creating jobs by constructing the highway system that still runs through that region. To aggressively seek to rebuild the economy of a devastated segment of America is hardly counter to our traditions; what runs counter to our traditions is the way that, today, we do *not* help.

Why should there *not* be a Marshall Plan for America's inner cities? It has been fifty years since America had a massive repair of its infrastructure. Our schools, parks, libraries, and highways all need a major overhaul. The whole country would benefit from a massive job-training and job-creation program for America's poor. What we lack is the political will to do it.

The pain of millions of Americans now stuck in a cycle of poverty and hopelessness can only result in greater social dysfunction, such as family rupture, drugs, and crime. More prisons and tougher welfare laws will of themselves do nothing but spray gasoline on the already raging fire. Hatred does not end hatred, and fear does not end fear.

A return to economic and social justice requires exertion of our national will. A massive focus on the economic revitalization of our poorer communities is, while not yet politically popular, morally correct. Some would say, "Well, they can get a job at McDonald's, if they want it," and that is a significant fact; but it does not substitute for providing a fair means to move beyond that job for those who are willing to exert the effort. People need more than jobs; they need the opportunity to get a good job. That is what job training and mass transit provide, and child care makes more possible. Underemployment is a crisis in America for millions of people. Child care is a crisis in America for millions of people. It is very important not to let low unemployment figures obscure the reality.

A conscience-based politics cares less for political expediency than for moral truth. We should extend our hands to the struggling portions of our nation for no other reason than that it is the right thing to do. Why would we bail out another country, but not our fellow Americans? And why would we not want to help those in trouble, if we ourselves are in our right minds?

ACCORDING to Thomas Jefferson, all Americans were to have universal access to the opportunity to produce modest material abundance. Not every rich person is greedy—by a long shot— any more than every poor person is kind and noble. Indeed, many of the richest Americans are becoming alarmed at the increasing economic disparities in America, for they do not bode well for any of us. If this boat sinks, we're all going down. It will do us little good to be wealthy if we have to live in gated communities and in fear for our very lives. That is what will happen in America if the emotional violence already spawned by economic injustice spills over into more widespread and collective expressions of outrage.

After World War I, the European Allies made a terrible mistake. Punishment of the vanquished Germans was cruel and unrelenting. U.S. President Woodrow Wilson passionately argued against the punishing attitude of our European Allies, predicting exactly what occurred: that an economically and socially crushed

Germany would be prey to something even more dangerous in the years ahead.

It is generally agreed by historians that if Germany had not been in such a desperate state in the years following World War I, Hitler would not have had such an easy rise to power. That is why we treated Germany and Japan so differently after World War II: we helped rebuild their economies, realizing finally that there is no greater threat to peace and security in the world than a large group of crushed and desperate people.

Should we not think on these things? Americans already employ more private than public police. Is this the direction in which we wish to keep moving?

We have to rethink money and its place in our lives if we are to transform American society. But the solution to economic injustice does not lie in making money bad. Spiritually, there is only one of us here; in the final analysis, there are no separate needs. Ultimately, what is good for Jesse Jackson is good for Rupert Murdoch. We do not have to choose between the rich and the poor, but only between consciousness of abundance and a consciousness of lack.

The primary political issue should not be the distribution of wealth but the creation of wealth. That is why job training, job creation, and education matter so much. The creation of wealth should be validated, not undermined; but it must be validated for *all* American citizens. It is not a limited amount of wealth, but a limited amount of creative, compassionate thinking that is our problem as a nation. There is not a limited amount of potential prosperity in America because there is not a limit to human creativity. In the presence of love, integrity, discipline, and the commitment to excellence, limits fade away.

President Kennedy said in his Inaugural Address, "The free society that does not take care of its many who are poor will not be able to save its few who are rich."

• • •

MEANWHILE, we continue to spend our tax dollars on those who need it least. We subsidize private California wineries, oil companies, timber and forest companies, the broadcasting industry, and others. We even gave McDonald's $1.6 million to help them advertise fast-food products overseas, and $78 million since 1986 to Sunkist so they could promote their oranges in Asia! With the latest tax bill we've agreed to pay $4 billion over the next ten years to subsidize ethanol, a gasoline substitute produced by Archer Daniels Midland. Last year, that company gave more than $1 million in political contributions to Democrats and Republicans. All of our subsidized industries, of course, are major election campaign contributors.

In the absence of campaign-finance reform, that's the way the system works.

CHANGE does not come from the top down, but from the bottom up. Each of us can help transform the financial ethos of the United States.

As individuals, and as a nation, we need to carefully watch our economic choices. They are powerful expressions of our values. Every time a screenwriter says, "No, I won't write a script in which the woman gets cut up into little pieces and the restaurant full of people gets blown away by a sixteen-year-old blonde bombshell carrying an Uzi, even if you do pay me $300,000," conscience takes an economic stand. Any time a lawyer says, "I won't let you buy my services so you can find a way to legally exploit old and feeble people out of their life savings," conscience takes an economic stand. Any time a business executive says, "I don't want to spend this meeting only asking ourselves how much money we're going to make, but how much good we're going to do for the country and the world this quarter," conscience takes an economic stand. Any time a lumber company executive says, "I don't care how much money we would get from cutting down those trees—we've only got 4 percent of our virgin forests left in this country as it is, and I don't want to steal from my grandkids anymore," conscience takes an economic stand. Any time a congressman says, "No I won't vote to take money away from summer job programs for inner-city youths and then vote *for* further subsidies for wealthy businesses that don't need it," conscience takes an economic stand.

A true marriage of conscience and economics will not depress the U.S. economy; it will rebuild it from within, revitalizing it in a way no external economic machinations could ever do. The greatest unmined source of wealth in America is the potential peace and happiness of millions of now stressed-out Americans. When we collectively return to our natural goodness, money will flow more easily for all of us. I heard a story once about a man who had some fishes and loaves. He told us to give to the poor. He always took care of the children. And he gave the money-changers a piece of His mind.

6

OLD POWERS, NEW POWERS

A L L abundance comes from within, as consciousness precedes matter. Our economic policy should be this: to teach and remind every American of his or her inestimable value and potential, to create the contexts in which those gifts are most easily mined, and then strictly adhere to the ethical standards by which each person is held accountable for what he or she does and does not do. Banks should not be at the center of our economic policy. The stock market should not be at the center of our economic policy. *We* should be at the center of our economic policy: our education, our welfare, our creativity, and our potential for genius.

We have been schooled in the ways of exploitation and greed. We were taught that this is the way to win, to sell the product, to get the ultimate reward. But the days are nearing an end when that kind of thinking will produce even a simulated version of abundance. It is thinking that is spiritually impoverished and will ultimately produce only material impoverishment.

The operative word in the phrase "wealth creation" is not *wealth* but *creation*. Our greatest untapped gold mine is the place within us where we learn to create material wealth out of the wealth of the spirit. And that we can't do by making money our goal, because the spirit will not be bought. While counterintuitive to current social wisdom, it is our purity and not our lack of it that is the key to manifesting wealth. It is a riddle, of course, because once you say, "Okay, so I'll be pure if that will make me more money," then you've lost your purity. Money comes from energy. That energy is like a magical bird that flies away from greed, overattachment, and lack of integrity. Working on our characters is the most powerful way now to work on our careers.

When I was in my twenties, I worked many jobs. At one point, I was scooping soup at Salmagundi's Restaurant in San Francisco. In walked a young man one day, an old friend I had not seen since high school, dressed in a pinstripe suit, out for lunch with his legal associates. He had been one of the smart kids at school, but so had I. I was traumatized to see him: I didn't want him to register the fact that while he was now a hot shot, I was scooping soup.

He was friendly to me, but there was pity on his face. I have never forgotten that moment.

For what had happened in Charles's life that had not happened in mine was that he figured out how to make it in America. I had fallen through the cracks, though that was not supposed to happen, given my family and background. I couldn't get myself to think the way I was told to think or move ahead in the ways I was supposed to move ahead. Yet I knew that day at Salmagundi's that I was carrying a diamond in my pocket. I hadn't gone to law school, but I had been traveling far and wide. I had experienced, while most of my friends were climbing ladders, realms of adventure that they thought they had to leave behind. I didn't know if I would ever get anywhere in the world, but I knew that there was an inner dimension to the life I was living that was brighter and cleaner than the world my friends were hailing as true success.

I have seen incredible things in my life, and one of them is that the spiritual diamond in my pocket became a key to success as the world defines it. Unknowingly, I had visited the void out of which comes overflowing materialization. That void, or no-thing, is the creative source of all abundance.

—

Internal abundance produces external abundance. That is true for an individual, and it is true for a nation. The life of the spirit is the source of all good.

ONE of the twentieth-century Wizards of Oz (he was a fraud, you remember; he *cannot* take you home) is the so-called science of economics. Economist Hazel Henderson has written, "Economics is now revealed as a 300-year-old grab bag of unverifiable propositions too vague to be refuted." Economists are like a group of people who came out of nowhere and all of a sudden run the world. Who made them boss? In the words of Mahatma Gandhi, "Nothing in history has been so disgraceful to the human intellect as the acceptance among us of the common doctrines of economics as a science." Economists do not normally include in their calculations such spiritual precepts as the Golden Rule, but the law of karma supersedes the laws of economics.

There are those who would say that to run a country with love in mind is not practical. But the argument that love is not *practical* is but a smokescreen. Of course, it is not practical. But what is practical? No one is saying love is practical, but only that it is *good*. Nowhere in the Bible, or in any other major spiritual source material that I have read, are we told to do what is practical. Would it take a lot of hours and debate and work and analysis to figure out how best to apply our resources toward the eradication of human suffering, here and throughout the world? Yes. Just about as many hours as it now takes figuring out how to wage espionage, create weapons of destruction, and produce the endless streams of things that we obsessively buy but do not need.

Love is as serious a subject, as difficult a subject, and as sophisticated a subject as money. Why should we treat economics more seriously than love? God is love, and love is the only abundance.

—

Everything else is just the toys we've been playing with at an immature level of our spiritual development.

From a spiritual perspective, no nation as wealthy as ours, with as many underprivileged children as we have, has any basis for long-term economic optimism whatsoever.

Doesn't love already rule the world, really? Isn't it love that makes people do what they think they could never do, and go where they thought they could never go? Is not nature wise, in its programming of mothers to instinctively love our children? Does this not guarantee the propagation of the species? Does not a tigress, or a lioness, grow fierce when she senses a threat to her cubs? Is not a species whose mothers are *not* so fiercely protective of their young unconsciously bent on its own destruction?

Our challenge now is to expand our concept of love and family to include the children on the other side of town. It is not enough to merely love our own children—so did slaveowners and Nazi officers. We must love all the children, here and throughout the world. To withhold love from them is to withhold support from the future, and time is speeding up now, literally.

As long as we stay resistant to a deeper, more penetrating discussion of the interior forces that rule the world, then our options for national recovery remain limited. Love will be allowed to save us, or violence will destroy us. Hatred cannot be endlessly managed, but it can, though the grace of God, be undone. It is overwhelmed, as is all darkness, in the presence of love. God's love is not separate from human love, because God is one. To understand that mystery, and to learn to live it, is the salvation of the human race. God is one, therefore you and I are one. God is one, therefore all nations are one. That is not a thought humanity has outgrown; it is a thought we have not yet quite grown deep enough to understand.

We must free the subject of love from the mental prison where it has been relegated by our pseudo-sophisticated bias. We must eschew the tacit injunction against its discussion in any other context but the romantic or the mundane. We are quickly coming upon an age when the question of what it means to love will define our science, our educational systems, indeed our politics. As the philosopher Pierre Teilhard de Chardin said, "Someday, after we have mastered the winds, the waves, the tides and gravity, we shall harness for God the energies of love. Then for the second time in the history of the world, man will have discovered fire."

IN 1997, some citizens in Oklahoma City created a project spearheaded by Oklahoma Supreme Court Justice Alma Wilson. It is called the Seeworth Preparatory School, and its mission is to address the problem of that state's "kids at risk." This means young people who don't make it in the public school system, who have gotten into either major or minor trouble and who, after being thrown out of school, usually find themselves sooner or later in jail.

Justice Wilson made a commitment to interrupting the destructive pattern in these children's lives. The system says it's "tried everything." Justice Wilson suggested we try love.

When I visited the Seeworth School, I spent some time with the students. Had I not already been told where these kids were from, what their previous histories had been, I would never have dreamed in a million years that these were the "bad kids" we hear about so often. They are clearly young people whose lives are being redeemed and restored, through the power of love and a discipline they can understand. Lisa told me she wants to be a lawyer, while Jennifer wants to be a physical therapist. Dylan wants to be a great psychologist, and Andrew wants to be a famous artist. Steven just wants his parents to love him.

The only problem with Seeworth Preparatory School is that

there are spaces for only 30 children, and it is currently dealing with a rate of 122 applicants for every slot. It is currently seeking to expand. The public school system allocates a minimal amount of money per student, and raising funds to keep the school afloat is left to private citizens. The task is difficult. The biggest problem, for all of us, is that there are literally millions of Jennifers and Andrews out there, with nowhere like that to go.

And yet everywhere I go, people respond enthusiastically to the story of the Seeworth Preparatory Academy. They can see the value of such a school in their own communities. Yet our government, beholden more to economic interests than to human interests, rarely reflects that kind of sensibility. Oh, they'll applaud it when it's a private effort, of course, but they are not apt in today's political climate to *fund* such an effort. We've got more important things to do with our money, such as buying additional C-130 cargo planes that the Pentagon didn't even ask for, to the tune of $422 million each. That part of the FY99 military budget was the work of Newt Gingrich before he left office, as the planes are manufactured in his hometown of Marietta, Georgia.

The truth is, our nation's children are simply not put first in America's collective consciousness today. Not really. Our continued withdrawal of support from our most disadvantaged communities only exacerbates the problems of kids at risk. And our fundamental response to kids in trouble now is simply to build more prisons. That is why prison building is our single largest urban industry, and our prison system is on its way to becoming the largest in the world.

In an interview in the *New York Times* in April 1997, former President Jimmy Carter cited inequities in the criminal justice system that often penalize black and other minority groups more than whites. He said that as a young governor of Georgia, he and his contemporaries, such as the then-governors of Florida and

Arkansas, had an intense competition over who had the smallest prison population.

"Now it's totally opposite," Mr. Carter added. "Now the governors brag on how many prisons they've built and how many people they can keep in jail and for how long."

Prison is, in fact, the beast's answer to Jennifer and Andrew. It is literally the only way that the two of them can currently contribute to the U.S. economy! It is not a mystery, what kids need in order to thrive. We know what they need in order to make it. But if their parents don't give it to them, our message to those kids in America today is "Tough breaks. You should have worked harder. It's really too bad."

And if we suggest that there are many people in America who could duplicate the Seeworth Preparatory School, at a lot less cost than what we now spend on prisons, we are liable to be met with lines such as, "Money doesn't solve these things," or "There you go again, talking about a big government program." But can you imagine what a major CEO would say if he or she budgeted funds for *infrastructure,* and you said that these things *just shouldn't cost money?* And why isn't the Pentagon looked at as a big government program—or the CIA, or corporate welfare?

THE number of local, state, and federal prisoners more than doubled in the last twelve years, with the prison population increasing by 56,000 in 1996 alone. While some say these statistics are a good thing because they prove that America's getting tougher on crime, there is a reality behind those statistics that bodes very badly for all of us.

While there are brilliant, dedicated individuals working within our criminal justice system, the attitudes beginning to dominate that system are barbaric. American society breeds hundreds of thousands of criminals, and then says to law enforcement, "Here, you handle it." We treat our prisons like garbage dumps to receive society's refuse. The problem of crime has become so huge in the United States that our government has opted for a crackdown mentality in its search for an illusory "safety." Then we get all these great new, wonderful crime statistics: crime is down! We got little Johnny on his first offense, see— which is great except that we'll have to deal with little Johnny again when he's *big* Johnny, who's just been let out of the prison where he was sodomized, beaten, and terrorized for ten years! Yippee!

In more and more states, there are statutes proposed to put young people in jail with the adult prison population. As a gentleman who works in juvenile justice said to me recently, wringing his hands and with tears in his eyes, "All I can say is, if you're going to treat these kids this way, then you better keep 'em in there a *really* long time."

What is going on behind bars in the United States today should be of serious concern to all of us. Even the significant minority who *want* criminals to suffer in prison would be horrified by reports of what is *really* going on there. Most Americans think of our prisons as at least humane, but there are increasingly terrible exceptions. Brutality is of epidemic proportions.

A sixteen-year-old schoolboy in Texas, named Rodney Hulin, Jr., was charged with arson in 1995, in a fire *that did $500 damage to a fence*. He admitted his guilt and was sentenced to *eight years in prison*. After having been repeatedly beaten and sexually assaulted during his first thirteen months in jail, during which he asked his father to pray for him that he would get out of prison alive, he hanged himself in his cell. From Georgia, there are reports of totally sadistic treatment of prisoners: men who had not violated any rules, or even resisted their guards, were handcuffed and had their faces and skulls crushed against walls by prison officials.

Do we plan to keep these people in jail forever? Or will we be dumping hundreds of thousands of men, women, and children onto our streets at the end of their prison sentences, and then reap whatever havoc one might reasonably expect on the part of those who have been, themselves, so brutalized?

If we do not change our direction drastically, then within five to fifteen years our cities will be like war zones. We will all be living in gated communities. We will travel in security police-protected caravans. We will shop only at private, guarded entertainment and shopping complexes. In other words, *we* will be in prison.

But we will have plenty of military equipment to protect our precious way of life and plenty of toys to keep us happy. Don't worry about it: none of *that* will be endangered.

In his farewell address to the nation, President Eisenhower said the following:

> We have been compelled to create a permanent armament's industry of vast proportions. . . .
>
> Now this conjunction of an immense military establishment and a large arms industry is new in the American experience. The total influence—economic, political, even spiritual—is felt in every city, every state house, every office of the Federal Government. We recognize the imperative need for this development. Yet we must not fail to comprehend its grave implications. Our toil, resources and livelihood are all involved; so is the very structure of our society.
>
> In the councils of Government, we must guard against the acquisition of unwarranted influence, whether sought or unsought, by the military-industrial complex. The potential for the disastrous rise of misplaced power exists and will persist.
>
> We must never let the weight of this combination endanger

our liberties or democratic processes. We should take nothing for granted. Only an alert and knowledgeable citizenry can compel the proper meshing of the huge industrial and military machinery of defense with our peaceful methods and goals, so that security and liberty may prosper together.

While Eisenhower's comments were made in the middle of the cold war, we clearly did not heed his warnings, either then or later. Since the end of the cold war, the global community is spending, on average, 30 to 40 percent less on military programs. Ours, however, remains at 82 percent of our cold war levels and consumes nearly 45 percent of all discretionary federal funds.

The United States today spends far more than the combined military budgets of all its potential adversaries (i.e., Russia, China, Iraq, Iran, North Korea, Libya, Cuba). While many believe that the current military budget is already out of proportion to the military threats in the world today—many say we could decrease it by a third without sacrificing the substance of our military preparedness—President Clinton, the Department of Defense, and members of Congress are planning to increase military spending by tens of billions of dollars over the next five years.

Americans seem convinced that we need the increase. Yet one wonders if people really know the facts. For the price of one B-2 bomber ($115 billion), which we're building even though the Pentagon doesn't want it, we could pay for the annual salaries of over 56,000 new elementary school teachers or 125,000 child-care workers.

Our elected officials are not so much protecting us here as robbing us. In 1953, alert to the dangers of a permanent armament's industry, President Eisenhower said, "Every gun that is made, every warship launched, every rocket fired signifies, in the final sense, a theft from those who are hungry and are not fed, those who are cold and are not clothed."

In truth, our military budget is more an expression of the financial appetites of our military-industrial complex than it is a truly wise response to admittedly very real threats to our national security. What could be a greater threat to our long-term security than the millions of American children who have no practical access to the social and cultural blessings of American society, and the millions of American adults finding it harder and harder to make ends meet while prosperity expands for so many others in more privileged parts of town?

While we currently face budget surpluses and unsurpassed economic prosperity, the Republican-led House of Representatives is proposing $26.3 billion of cuts in domestic spending in the year 2000. The cuts will come in spending categories covering education, job training, housing, health and human services, environmental protection, care for our veterans, medical and technological research, and diplomacy and foreign aid, among other Federal programs. These follow $53 billion in cuts in domestic spending since the Republicans won control of Congress in 1994.

Meanwhile, while domestic spending will decrease, our military spending will *increase* by $18.9 billion. Of the $538 billion budget pie left after paying for mandatory programs like Medicare, Congress is appropriating $270 billion—*more than half the money*—to the Defense Department. Every other Government agency, covering all the issues listed above, will receive an aggregate of about $268 billion. Military spending will go up 7.5 percent, and domestic spending will go down 11 percent next year. In percentage terms, this represents the lowest domestic spending levels since 1962.

What is happening when a nation is so much more willing to fund its vengeance than its compassion? Is there something wrong with the American soul? Not really. Our soul is intact; we are basically a decent and compassionate people. The problem is that our government does not reflect that. It is ruled for the most part not by the "better angels" of the American people, but by the gargantuan economic interests of a relatively few industries. Until that changes—until a massive shift in American consciousness turns the American mind back to the political process, demanding the place we were intended to have within it, demanding campaign-finance reform, demanding that special economic interests no longer be the primary architects of our social and political policy—our own goodness will continue to be less and less reflected in the actions taken in our name. That is the basic healing America needs: not to find its soul, but to *live* its soul. Our souls must be allowed to express themselves in circles of influence wider than just our private domains.

It is time for us to ask ourselves, "Is it possible to have a compassion-based society?" "What would such a society look like?" and "What changes need to take place in our public policies if our goal as a society is to express love instead of fear?"

Perhaps you wish to write your elected officials and tell them that you prefer to have your tax dollars fund the goals of peace more than the machinery of war. Just writing that letter will make a difference inside you. And someone on the other end will read it.

Remember this from *A Course in Miracles:* "A miracle is never lost. It may touch many people you have not even met, and produce undreamed of changes in situations of which you are not even aware."

The American people aren't happy with the fact that money runs Washington more than we do. We just don't know what to do about it. We don't know who to turn to when both major political parties are so beholden to corporate interests. We don't know how to express our rage, and so it shows up in our midst as apathy or denial. That is why the assumption of spiritual power is so important as a political tool.

Meanwhile, an American is less likely to die from a nuclear bomb today than from a suitcase full of nerve gas left on a downtown street anywhere in America. The actual threats to our security lie more in the form of chemical and biological warfare and domestic terrorism than in traditional military warfare, and all the trillions of dollars we are spending on the latter have very little to do with the most serious threats to our national security at this time.

Do we need a military? Of course we do. Do we need to radically rethink its function and its operation? Maybe we should think about that. Perhaps it would behoove us to ask ourselves why we are so disliked by many people around the globe. What relatively little money (.6 of 1 percent of our budget) we do give to nations less fortunate than we is applied far less to humanitarian than to military use, or to prop up multinational corporate regimes that primarily serve our own economic interests. For all our talk about how generous we are, the United States has become one of the most miserly countries in the world. It is not just the nuclear bombs pointing in our direction, but all the enmity pointed in our direction, that should make every American pause and think. As one expert on chemical warfare was quoted as saying, "The only way the United States could really be safe from the threat of chemical warfare is if there weren't so many people out there who hated us."

In the century now dawning, spirituality, visionary consciousness, and the ability to build and mend human relationships will be more important for the fate and safety of this nation than our capacity to forcefully subdue an enemy. Creating the world we want is a much more subtle but more powerful mode of operation than destroying the one we don't want.

We spend trillions of dollars on methods of destroying life, while routinely withdrawing millions of dollars from projects and efforts to restore life.

In *A Course in Miracles*, it is written that we create what we defend against. Apply that to our military establishment, and perhaps we have a problem here. The protection afforded us by the machinations of America's war machine will serve us but little, if we do not address the fundamental causes of hatred and violence, here and throughout the world. We need a Department of Peace, at least as much as we need a Department of Defense.

THERE will be no real peace in the world until there is peace in our hearts. And in both places, there is a big difference between the creation of true peace and mere management of the symptoms of distress.

One of the ways that we are bordering on cultural insanity, in a dysfunctional effort to suppress our pain rather than truly heal ourselves, is in the area of drugs. A system that makes a lot of noise about battling drugs is itself invested in our being stoned.

While our politicians are big on discussing America's drug problem, they hardly ever discuss sobriety. There is a reason for this: sobriety doesn't yet play a serious part in mainstream conversation because America hasn't yet decided to become sober. The most significant drug stash in America is in our collective medicine chests. America has become a legally ordained drug culture.

Americans act these days as though taking a prescription drug is not really taking drugs, which is much like saying that using a credit card isn't really spending money. Our mass consumption of legalized chemicals should show us how oddly selective we are in our condemnation of drugs.

Legal, though not necessarily morally legitimate, pharmaceutical company campaigns have set out to drug America, with far too many doctors as their willing accomplices. We drop antidepressants like candy, often giving them to our teenagers for no better reason, from what I can see, than that the kid is acting like a teenager. I can't imagine Beaver Cleaver's mother looking at the antics of one of her sons and saying, "Oops, that's a case of obsessive-compulsive disorder if I ever saw one! Dope him up."

America's overmedication of itself and its children is our biggest "dirty little secret." Notice how illegal drugs are called drugs, but legal drugs are called "medication." "So-and-so thinks I should go on medication" has replaced what we used to say in the old days: "Do you know where I can get a gram?" "My doctor prescribed it" has replaced "I'm not addicted—I just do it every once in a while."

The kid's a problem? Attention deficit disorder? Put him on Ritalin. Can't deal with the pressure of work and home? Prozac might be the answer. Official estimates place anywhere from 5 to 15 percent of America's approximately 39 million schoolchildren on regular antidepressants. It is no surprise that the United States accounts for 90 percent of the world's Ritalin use. Particularly shocking is the way we often abuse our own children with drugs in an effort to make them docile and easy to manage, rather than making the effort to find other ways of meeting their needs. We are encouraging an entire generation of young people to rely on psychiatric drugs rather than on themselves and other human resources—not to even mention God. Clearly we are having some problems of our own when we are so quick to drug our own kids.

I'm not saying that there are never legitimate reasons for psychiatric drugs, because there clearly are. But the bigger issue is America's hypocrisy in not facing up to our addictive patterns, preferring to suppress the symptoms rather than legitimately deal with our pain. We have allowed billion-dollar industries to grow up around ways to manage and suppress our misery.

Psychologist Carl Jung said, "All neurosis is a substitute for legitimate suffering." As a culture, America lacks a deep understanding of the value of suffering. Contrary to popular opinion, there are times when allowing ourselves to suffer is the only way to get through the pain.

American popular culture is a cult of pleasure, which is an inappropriate response to deep unhappiness. The happiest life is an authentic life, which is not necessarily one of constant delight. Our obsessive pursuit of entertainment and cheap pleasure is both a response to and a masking of deep unhappiness. When, after fifteen minutes, the pain comes back—no matter how much fun we had and how many games we bought—we should do more than just seek to numb it.

It's important that our bones hurt when we break them. Otherwise, how would we know that they're broken? But if you have a broken bone, you don't just take painkillers; you have to reset the bone. So it is with our society: the fact that so many of us endure deep psychic pain on a daily basis—one in four women in America will be diagnosed as clinically depressed—should be something more significant than a gold mine for drug manufacturers. It should be the source of deep questioning regarding what has gone so wrong and the embrace of real solutions—*like maybe a serious spiritual life.* Why is a pharmaceutical company that makes billions of dollars manufacturing antidepressants called a legitimate capitalist concern, but someone who suggests that we pray and meditate regularly to help treat depression liable to be called a snake-oil salesman?

Americans don't need to *treat* our unhappiness so much as we need to *respond* to it. Unhappiness is here for a reason; it is trying to tell us something. It is a sign that who we have been in our

lives, and what we have been doing with our lives, is an inadequate container for the energies trying to emerge within us. Usually it is a sign that on some level we have been playing way too
powerless; responding to that powerlessness with drugs is like
saying that we'll respond to a cut by cutting ourselves again.

Our war against drugs is odd, at best. It's basically a prohibi-
tion that hasn't worked, undertaken by a society that is itself addicted to drugs. I think we keep fighting the drug war for that
reason: like any addict, we try to deflect attention away from our
own use. The criminal underclass created by the "drug war" costs
America more in lives and money and outright human tragedy
than any straight-out use of the outlawed drugs ever would if
they were legal. Even more important, our children, in taking
drugs, are far too often merely imitating us.

If we were intent on fighting drugs in this country, we would
seriously foster recovery. We would have twelve-step recovery
meetings in the high schools during the afternoons. I've heard
that a Recovery Channel is going to start broadcasting on television soon; for a fraction of the money we spend fighting drugs,
we could have federally funded such a network years ago.

And most important, we should begin asking ourselves what
the hole is inside our children, and inside us, that we are all seeking to fill so dysfunctionally? What is it about the world we have
created for ourselves that we so don't want to *be* here?

Saying that we are going to win the war on drugs is like saying
that we'll get rid of the Viet Cong. Damned if there wasn't always another one right behind that next tree. So there will be
drugs on our streets, no matter how much money we spend trying to stop them, as long as there is a spiritual wound in the gut
of America's children. And there will be that pain in them until
we have adequately addressed the pain in us.

The issue is a paradigmatic one: we are on the verge of outgrowing a mind-set that says "I will deal with this problem by say-ing no to something" and embracing one that says "I will deal with this problem by saying *yes* to something else." Notice we have a Drug Czar, but not a Sobriety Czar. It's as though our government is run by a group of old-fashioned father figures who rarely spend any time at home, but then love to come into the house and start giving orders. The kids look at him like he's crazy. Who's done more to get America off drugs—Gerald Ford or Betty Ford?

Our drug war should be replaced by a national sobriety cam-paign. And that means a whole lot more than just saying no; it means saying yes to some things that America, deep in its heart, has not yet decided it wants to say yes to.

The only way America is going to solve its drug problem is if we retrieve our spiritual awareness. That is what sobriety is. There is a magic within each of us that we consistently deny, because it lies in the realm of the imagination. We have been trained since child-hood to view the imagination as a less important function than the intellect. This has left us emotionally and spiritually bereft. Tak-ing drugs is a desperate effort to compensate for the loss.

The most dangerous thing in the world for a free society is for a critical mass of people to lose conscious contact with the place within us that says, "Hey, something's fishy here. I feel something rotten in my gut." Not everything that is happening in America today would make a person who is in his or her right mind happy: that's why we have to *be* in our right minds. Our right minds are our salvation.

THERE is something about having a child that makes a woman feel she's a member of the universal "Mommy Club." It's not just my own child, but every child, who seems so critically important to me now that I'm a mother.

I know that the mothers of America care about the state of our nation's children. But we are so oddly quiet, so sadly co-opted by the forces that threaten them. Even female hyenas encircle their children, making sure that the adult males cannot feed until the cubs have had a chance to. Surely the women of America can do better than the hyenas.

The true mother archetype is not just soft; she is fierce. And this feminine archetype is making a dramatic new appearance in modern consciousness. She opens a psychic curtain to reveal a radically different worldview than our own, where the female is freed from age-old prejudice and expresses her total nature without fear.

Part of her total nature is to protect her children at all costs. It is *unnatural* the way American women are acquiescing to the assaults on America's children today. As animals protect their feeding offspring, should we not protect our own? Today's food supply is increasingly placed at risk from all manner of carcinogenic content, while American women are still too uninformed, or too distracted, to cry "Foul" in any meaningful way.

I think both sexes will cry "Foul" when Americans wake up to the dangers of genetically engineered food and its prevalence among us.

MANY of the most forward-thinking social thinkers in the world today believe that the largest crisis looming in our future could well be in the area of food. Large American biotech companies control the majority of food-production processes, not only in the United States but increasingly throughout the world. Over the past two years, the United States (particularly giants Monsanto and Dow) has flooded the world market with unregulated and unlabeled genetically engineered grain, a practice that Europeans and others in the international community are resisting fiercely. Early in March of 1999, the United States and four of its allies sabotaged a treaty agreed upon by 131 other countries, which would have forced all food exporters to label genetically engineered food being sent to another nation.

This is an example where the right to trade, to make money, to expand markets, is placed before safety, protocol, or ethics of any sort. It is blossoming into a huge issue in this country and around the world, and the Monsanto Corporation, particularly, is making decisions about our food supply that normally one would think people themselves should be making. If I don't want my child to eat something that has been produced through genetic engineering—the cross-breeding of genes from one plant or species with another—then shouldn't I have the right to make that decision? Shouldn't any mother anywhere have that right? Shouldn't we at least have the right to *know* what we're eating?

Or is Monsanto simply more important?

There is a growing awareness among Americans of the potentially grave dangers of genetically engineered products, and the labeling of items containing those products is now a hot political issue. From recombinant Bovine Growth Hormone—administered to dairy cows to increase milk production even though independent research demonstrates that this hormone raises the level of an insulinlike growth factor that has been linked to human cancer (Canada has banned the use of the hormone)—to the splicing of genes from bacteria into potatoes, tomatoes, and even into the soy and corn that is used in infant formula, a critical mass of public concern is finally beginning to emerge. Pressure is being put on both the White House and Congress to put advocacy for the American consumer before advocacy for the biotech industry. Since the *New York Times* reported in May 1999 that Monarch butterflies have been dying after being exposed to genetically engineered corn, people have increasingly started to ask themselves why the safety of our children is not receiving higher priority in Washington.

According to the Council for Responsible Genetics, "The FDA has shrugged its responsibility for regulating genetically engineered foods . . . a precautionary 'safety proven first' policy has been scrapped in favor of corporate economic interests." While a "revolving-door policy" in Washington, D.C., has made it common for government employees to leave their jobs and go to work for the companies they have been regulating, and vice versa, government officials at the highest levels are finally beginning to hear the cries of "Foul" coming in by phone, letter, and e-mail from all around the country.

Genetically engineered products should be labeled as such. If you agree with that view, it is a very, very good idea to call or write your Congresspeople and tell them so. This is one more area where it behooves us to remember that our government officials hear from corporate lobbyists every single day. It is not enough for them to hear from you and me only once every two or four years.

YANG, or externalized activism, has defined politics in the age now passing; yin, internalized activism, will be a political force in the age now dawning. Soul force emanates subtle energies that invisibly move and heal the world. Soul force is the essence of a new politics because it consists of the social energies released when a sleeping population awakens. Democracy cannot survive a continuing and growing mass of people who either do not care what happens, are not looking at what happens, or do not act on what they feel about what is happening. We can have a nap or we can have freedom. We cannot have both.

Too much shopping is a way we lull ourselves to sleep. Too much television is a way we lull ourselves to sleep. Drug and alcohol use is a way we lull ourselves to sleep. Too much petty conversation is a way we lull ourselves to sleep. And, meanwhile, we want to go to sleep because we are basically depressed. We are depressed because we're not doing what we came here to do. As Americans, we have awesome power to make this world a better place. Somewhere in our souls we know this. Somewhere in our souls we want this. And somewhere in our souls we are looking for a way to break through to the place where we are fully alive.

Women have a special connection to inner worlds, though that connection has been violently torn asunder for centuries. During the Middle Ages, every feudal village in Europe had a group of women called the witches—literally meaning "wise women." They were the herbalists, midwives, and healers of their world. They facilitated community rituals, which held the inhabitants of a village in sacred connection to nature, each other, and themselves. They held a space, as it were, for the individual's sense of personal connection to the divine. Some of them were called hags. The word *hag* originally meant "mature woman who carries sacred knowledge."

The witch burnings of the Middle Ages were a systematic effort by the early church to eradicate the passionate, freethinking woman. Why? Because such women tended to raise passionate, freethinking children. And such children tended to become passionate, freethinking adults. Passionate, freethinking adults are very difficult to manipulate and almost impossible to control. Any time a group or institution seeks to gain control over human minds, one of its first attacks is on passionate women.

What do witch trials have to do with modern America? A lot. There is in modern Western women a cellular memory of burning at the stake, just as there is in modern American blacks a cellular memory of slavery. Many women today are still afraid to speak their piece, and there are those who feel it the most natural thing in the world to burn us when we do.

Yet if the women of America were to speak our hearts, this country would explode in light. Gandhi once said, "If I could awaken the women of Asia, I could free India in a day."

Several male clergy have been respectfully referred to as President Clinton's spiritual advisers, but author and scholar Jean Houston's career, after consulting with Mrs. Clinton, was undermined by lies and innuendo. Her prodigious intellect was trivialized, and a standard Gestalt technique she used in her work was irresponsibly called a "seance." As Houston said regarding her accuser, "Mr. Woodwind confuses the fringe with the frontier." We have so dumbed down the entire culture that anything that doesn't fit into the white-bread section of the supermarket is deemed way too controversial for America to handle.

That is very sad for all of us, because the nourishment we most need will not come from white bread. We need expanded frontiers of knowledge, new sets of questions, and a more sacred, piercing sensibility. We are comfortable with male ministers being at the White House because we know what they're saying there; *they stay within the boxes.* But the man who announced in the light of day his need for male ministers was tended to in his darker moments by mature women of spirit, and that is fact.

Actually, if more spiritually mature feminine forces had been invited to enter through his front door, perhaps such an immature one would not have had to slip in through the back.

WHAT do so many of us wish to bring back to civilized awareness in a more potent, alive way? Mystery, intuition, ritual, relationship, healing, emotion, soul, community, imagination. Important parts of who we all are. The stuff of magic and magical people.

The people who never dropped those things from the forefront of their consciousness are the people who have lived at the margins of power in Western civilization during the era now drawing to a close. They have been suppressed at the deepest level, not because the prevailing patriarchal consciousness thought that they were *less* than. They were repressed because, unconsciously, it was suspected that they were *more* than. All people, through the grace of God, have mystical power greatly underutilized in this now-passing millennium, but it is people who have been historically held down, whose inner strengths have been simmering within the pressure cooker of their profound long suffering, who now stand at the forefront of humanity's rebirth.

The following stanza from G. K. Chesterton's poem "The Secret People" is one of my favorite expressions of how the magic of the soul has been shoved aside in the consciousness of the modern world:

> They have given us into the hand of the new unhappy lords,
> Lords without anger and honour, who dare not carry their
>   swords.
> They fight by shuffling paper; they have bright dead alien
>   eyes;
> They look at our labour and laughter as a tired man looks
>   at flies.
> And the load of their loveless pity is worse than the ancient
>   wrongs,
> Their doors are shut in the evening; and they know no songs.

The magic people—of both sexes and all races—haven't been invited to attend the party in America, for fear that they might dance. They haven't been invited to speak at the party, for fear that they might sing. They haven't been invited to run the party, for fear that they might change it.

They would have, and now they're going to. They are the

spirit of a new America, and a key to the revitalization of our democracy.

There has always been a divine plan for the destiny of this nation. Something of indescribable power and light is brewing among us now. It will take us back to the path of the heart, and God Himself will lead us on from there.

7

HOLISTIC
POLITICS

B E Y O N D the appearances of history, there is a great and glorious unfolding plan for the destiny of nations. According to the mystical traditions, God carries this plan within His mind, seeking always, in every way, channels for its furtherance. His plan for the evolution of humanity, and the preparation of teachers to guide it, is called within the esoteric traditions the Great Work.

Contribution to this work is not unique to any one nation or people. On every continent, in every age, there have been spectacular contributions made to humanity's journey toward the fullness of our being. Worldly institutions are useful in advancing God's plan for the enlightenment of the world, to the extent to which the ideals of that institution reflect the highest philosophical truths. The Declaration of Independence, the U.S. Constitution, and other great beams of American light have reflected and furthered the evolutionary arc of humanity's progress.

Yet no mortal, and no nation made up of mortals, is immune to pride or ego or selfishness or greed. Where immoderate ambition or brute power take hold, the fragile bond is broken between the spirit of the Great Work and the structure that contained it. The Work continues; it always continues. But it leaves behind what becomes unworthy of it and gravitates toward truer hearts.

In modern sociological terms, there is a phenomenon called the "local discontinuity of progress." The next step forward in a system rarely comes from a predictable place. Grace is not logical, nor can brilliant insight be rationally formulated. Where human beings pride themselves, the spirit of God departs. Human arrogance is not a container for God, nor will it ever be.

When a particular group or structure fails to keep faith with the spirit of love—not measured by its words but by its actions— that structure then loses the privilege of guardianship of the great Work. The plan passes on to other groups or structures. Human beings cannot stop or pervert the work of destiny, but we can dissociate ourselves from its higher unfoldment. Having done so, then we will cease to share in its blessings.

America has been a vessel for the great Work from its inception. Now, however, we have in many ways lost our conscious contact with the greatness of our destiny. We ignore invisible principles yet obsess about all manner of visible pursuits. We allow our time and attention to be frittered away in a scramble for things too shallow to satisfy us even if we can attain them. Having overcome so many forms of external dysfunction, we are now bound up by internal ones.

But powers greater than we continue to minister to humanity. Today, as always, any heart or institution that surrenders itself becomes a channel for the vibrations of love still emanating from the mind of God. It is never too late to change our minds, to self-correct, to embrace the notion that all men are brothers, that indeed we are One, that what we do to anyone we are doing to ourselves, and that in time we will come to see this and know this and live this in truth.

America keeps trying to find the right drivers, when instead we should be questioning what road we're on. Contrary to what we are told, the road that we are currently on is not full of just light; the road ahead is full of consequences. But there is another road that America can take, a road of high and enlightened purpose for both our abundance and our genius.

Material expansion will take care of itself if we take care of all
things true and beautiful. For those whose hearts respond to this
thought, it is time to break through the superstitious thinking that
might lead us to believe it's too late to change. We can change, we
will change—in fact, we are changing. That is our destiny. A
question that faces us is this: can we recreate politics and society
to reflect these things, or must the pursuit of higher truth remain
separate from the public sphere? This moment is one of opportunity for the creation of a new civic forcefield. It is up to each and
every one of us to decide where America goes now.

WITH the impeachment of President Clinton and his ensuing
trial in the Senate, the United States concretized our now near
total split between what we call politics and what politics might
mean in an enlightened environment. Where is a political context for higher questioning, for national self-definition beyond
economic and military power, for national purpose beyond increasing our economic status, for national compassion of any
kind at all? The question of whether President Clinton lied is not
unimportant, but neither should be the question of whether government agencies lie in order to make it easier for corporate giants to place known carcinogens in our water, our food, and the
air we breathe, threatening our health while increasing their
short-term profits. The question of whether President Clinton
obstructed justice is not unimportant, but neither should be the
question of whether the World Trade Organization, or GATT,
or the International Monetary Fund obstruct economic justice in
this country and throughout the world. The question of whether
the President is morally fit for office is not unimportant, but neither is the question of whether our entire government is morally

fit for office, if it doesn't even *try* to fundamentally redress the rampant economic and social inequalities in our society today.

In business, for the most part, there is an inherent motivation to serve people. In government, owing to the extraordinary pernicious influence of money on the electoral process (an influence which will not abate, by the way, until campaign finance reform is enacted by the U.S. Congress), this is no longer necessarily true. The interests of "the people" are often secondary to the interests of major political contributors. Those who see economics as the primary determinant of our "vital interests" aren't always looking for the loving solution to domestic or international problems. If love came first, we would use our financial resources to create jobs to help people live well, instead of building more prisons to punish them when they do not; if love came first, we would value human rights at least as much as economic rights; if love came first, we would seek to educate and help rather than to prosecute our children violently screaming out for attention.

Yet what are the great political issues of our time? For a while it was whether or not the stain on the blue dress matched President Clinton's DNA, and now it's morphed for the moment into what we do with Social Security, taxes, or Medicare. Meanwhile, much more fundamental questions rage whether we are asking them or not.

- *Fundamental question:* The way we're now threatening our biosphere, the question within twenty or thirty years might be far more critical than whether our Social Security checks arrive; it might be whether or not we have irreparably damaged the environment to the point of arousing violent competition for food and water throughout the world in the years ahead.

- *Fundamental question:* Do we, as a nation, really want to be a small portion of the world's population consuming the lion's share of the world's resources, calling our absolute right to do so our "vital national interest," thus sowing seeds for our own inevitable comeuppance some time in the century ahead?
- *Fundamental question:* Should American power drive the financial engines of the world, pushing more and more corners of the planet in the direction of uncontrolled economic growth while, in fact, the natural resources of the earth are already maxed out?
- *Fundamental question:* Are we content responding to the rage and despair of millions of underprivileged Americans with an ever more lucrative system of punishment rather than a committed system of education and economic revitalization?
- *Fundamental question:* What is the state of American democracy itself, with the continuing tide of the disengagement of our people from the political process? Are we not nervous that in the 1998 elections, only 11 percent of newly eligible young voters even chose to the go the polls, feeling as cynical as they obviously do about the process?

These are important questions, of course. Yet we settle for a political milieu where what is important, even critical to our survival as a species, is often deemed a marginal concern, and what is trivial is often deemed the hot news of the day.

THE question before us is: how do people who have reclaimed their spirituality best effect political change? We have already established that only nonviolent resistance is acceptable to the spiritual seeker, and ultimately it is the only kind of resistance that is truly effective anyway. When a power dominates the physical world, it is in looking beyond the physical world that we find our victory.

Just as David took on the giant Goliath, there is an emerging gestalt of spiritually based activism around the world, ready and willing to form a wave of resistance to multinational corporate dominance of the planet and its peoples. As usual, Goliath is bigger than we are. As usual, Goliath is totally armored and defended. As usual, Goliath laughs at his critics. As usual, Goliath taunts his enemies.

But consider this as well: as usual, Goliath moves slowly. As usual, Goliath is not as smart as he thinks he is. As usual, Goliath's Third Eye is uncovered; one hit in the middle of his forehead, and the giant will go down. Make his conscience your bull's-eye, and he cannot help but transform.

The evil, as well as the ultimate vulnerability of the giant, is that it is not human. Its life force is not the spirit at the center of the universe, but merely corporate papers filed away somewhere, in Delaware or wherever. A corporate entity is not a human. Of itself it has no heart or soul or conscience. It cannot cry, or fall in love, or conceive a child, or feel pain. That is what makes it dangerous, and also what makes its days so numbered. A force that is not *alive* is now ruling the world, and nature will not endure that forever.

To be sure, there are human beings who run that corporate machinery, but they themselves are often slaves to its functioning. I've been told by corporate CEOs who fully agreed with me in theory that their policies were at least potentially threatening to the planet and its peoples, "Marianne, I know what you're saying, but I'm answerable to my stockholders. If I bungle it this quarter and don't increase their bottom line, I'll be out, and the person who replaces me will probably be worse than me." To others, unfortunately, all that matters is the value of their own stock options at the point of their retirement. Until stockholders make it clear to corporate powers that we don't want our investments to yield financial profit at the expense of the quality of human lives, then many corporations will continue to place economic values before human ones, and all of us will harvest the results of our collective sins at a later date.

Corporations aren't made up of evil people, and corporations aren't inherently evil. Far from it. And there are thousands of people around the country and the world, doing brilliant, transformative work on changing the human ethos of the large corporation. Socially responsible investing is growing in leaps and bounds.

What is potentially evil, wherever it is found, is placing money before people. And most corporations are not in the business of serving people, except to the extent that serving people then in turn serves the corporation. That is why a huge, multinational corporate presence, wielding immoderate economic power, is such a threat to democracy and justice everywhere. At a certain point in life, we have to decide what matters to us most as individuals and as a society. And unless what matters most is human beings, we will ultimately suffer. Our bottom line should be love and not money.

The person of conscience, deeply committed to a radical change in human civilization—from a dangerous, unsustainable social order to a veritable garden for our children and grandchildren—must be willing to risk being considered a whiner by polite society. The nonviolent revolutionary has a responsibility to be a thorn in the side of a complacent status quo. The person of conscience holds up a mirror to the world, which must include him or herself. The lover of humanity is an agent of awakening, in a world where there is a collective urge to sleep.

Why should news programs have daily reports on how Wall Street is doing but not on how our children are doing? Why are we to be more concerned, as a society, if the stock market is depressed than if our *people* are depressed? Why is the fact that an American teenager is sixteen times more likely to die of gun violence than are the children of the twenty-five largest industrial nations in the world not even a *topic* in political campaigns, unless a tragedy just happens to have occurred the week before? Why does the military garner so much support and our poor so little? Why is money given so much more respect than children? And who is going to change the public conversation from shallow economic inanity to passionate human concern, if not you and me?

It is true that in many environments, to bring up the unnecessary suffering of millions—and the policies that perpetuate that suffering—might quickly get you slapped with a label of "bleeding heart." But there's an answer to that: *be slapped*. Be slapped over and over. And take heart. All you need is one person in the room to say, "Actually, I agree with that," and we're starting to act like participants in a broad-based social change.

Just saying those things is not enough, of course; there is much more we need to do than just talk. But once the words have left your mouth, they tend to be more alive within you.

Anthropologist Margaret Mead gave us a perfect slogan for such times as these: "Never doubt that a small group of concerned citizens can change the world," she said. "Indeed, it is the only thing that ever has."

FROM corporate agricultural giants turning the American farmer into an economic serf, to the injection of all manner of potentially dangerous chemical and genetic elements into our food production processes merely to increase corporate profits, to the displacement of people throughout the world to smaller and smaller corridors of economic and social opportunity when they no longer serve the machinery of international financial institutions, to the suppression of democratic protests against such economic dominance, to a system of corporate welfare that makes it so much easier for the rich to do business in America than for the poor to even get started, Americans are seeing things that are clearly antithetical to the ideals on which this nation was founded.

We hear true righteous indignation rising up from neither the Democratic nor Republican political machinery, beholden as they both are to corporate money. But our indignation is rising nonetheless, and the chains that now seemingly bind our national conscience will be overthrown in some miraculous way, because David could sing and David had a slingshot and David loved the Lord his God with all his heart and all his might. He knew that "the Lord saves not with sword and spear." The Lord saves with love, as all of us know in the depths of our souls. We must love the oppressed and we must love the oppressor, but we must refuse to participate in the oppression itself. We must name the game, tell truth to power, and lift above the battlefield not in anger but in love, not in fear but in hope, not in cynicism but in absolute conviction that here, in these United States, we have always risen to the challenge of justice, and now, in our day, we will do the same. The game isn't over. It has only just begun. We *do* love justice more than we love our designer brand tennis shoes; we *do* love our children enough to make a stand for their safety against the environmental encroachments of an invisible order; and we *do* love America enough to turn our attention back to politics and reclaim that realm for our most honorable impulses, compassionate feelings, and noble thoughts.

Watch out, Goliath, once America wakes up and sees what's happening. There's a storm ahead, or an awakening ahead. Let's embrace the awakening and choose lessons in joy instead of lessons in pain. One way or the other, the lessons are coming. The spirit will not be held down, in the century up ahead.

• • •

—

PLATO said that "to philosophize and concern oneself with politics is one and the same thing." We expand our political activism to include spiritual growth work, in order that we might ourselves become facilitators of change. And we expand our perception of spiritual practice to include political activism, that we might most profoundly extend our compassion into the world.

A path of love takes conscious effort. Many Americans have the unfortunate habit of waking up every morning and surrendering their lives to fear. Newspapers, radio or TV news, caffeine or nicotine get hold of our nervous systems and hook us into the anxiety-ridden miasma we call contemporary culture before we're even out the door.

The cultivation of hallowed silence, meditation, or prayer; even a small amount of inspirational literature, a minimum amount of yoga or centering exercise—these are things that counter the fear and help to lift us above the realm of our popular hysteria. *After* we meditate, we're ready to read the paper; after we're inspired, we're better prepared to be informed.

Politics can be a tremendous temptation to stray from our spiritual center. One newspaper piece about abandoned kids, and we're angry. One bill passed in Congress because of unfair special interest influence, and our judgmental mind goes off the charts. The ego within us loudly proclaims both our anger and our fear. No louder voice, but only silence itself, can stop the noise within. What we most need to hear today, we can only hear when the mind is quiet.

Devotional silence is a powerful tool for healing hearts and healing nations; as any of us grow closer to God, all of us grow closer to each other. That can be difficult to see sometimes, with the rise of certain so-called religious groups throughout the world that clearly separate more than divide us. But the true experience of God, through love and forgiveness, unites instead of separates. Now, an international grassroots movement—made up of people from all religions and no religions—is gathering in spirit to forge an experience of universal oneness. This experience—unorganized, spontaneous, international, and inspired—will ultimately join all hearts.

POWER doesn't flow from the top down, but from the bottom up. Wisdom doesn't flow from the outside in, but from the inside out. Both of those spiritual tenets are at the core of a highly functioning democratic process. Where a top-down, authoritarian power holds sway, democracy is diminished. Where people get their guidance only from external sources, as opposed to the goodness of our own hearts, democracy is diminished as well. Disconnection from our internal selves produces a decrease in personal energy, or *chi,* and where personal energy diminishes, the last thing we feel we have time for is participation in the democratic process. Tired people don't *do* democracy, and that is why a distracted, burdened, overstressed population is literally a threat to our liberty. President Eisenhower said, "Politics should be the part-time profession of every American." But tell that to someone who already *has* two part-time jobs!

One of the ways to reconnect our personal and political energy is through a project called Citizen Circles. These are small, grassroots groups held all around the country, in which two or more join together to hold the vision of a healed America.* To "hold a vision" is to hold a thought, and thought is the most powerful, creative force in the universe. We are, as a species, only beginning to tap into the true power of our spiritual imagination—the wings we have been given but have not yet begun to collectively use. A thought grows more powerful the more peo-

*For more information regarding Citizen Circles, see page 263.

ple hold it. "An invasion of armies can be resisted," wrote Victor Hugo, "but not an idea whose time has come." The Berlin Wall came down because the love of freedom literally overcame the physical and political structures that resisted it. We, too, can make a bloodless transition to a better social order. We can so consciously embrace a world of justice and compassion, that such a world will literally be magnetized into manifestation. Such is the miraculous power of the human heart.

Citizen Circles open with a prayer or inspirational quote, remaining both religiously and spiritually inclusive. Twenty minutes of silence follow. For some people this is a time for prayer or meditation, while for others it is merely a time for personal reflection. Our wisdom, being rooted in silence, is then more clearly brought to bear upon our social and political lives.

It is written in the Bible, "Be still and know I am." There is a power in stillness to counter the cacophonous, hysterical energy that dominates so much of our popular culture today. Sharing silence in groups is a powerful way, in the words of Gandhi, to help "make politics sacred." At the beginning of the devotional silence is a Quaker-type exercise, in which those who feel so moved say, "I see an America in which . . .", followed by their vision of a healed nation. We might see a nation or world in which all children are safe and happy and educated. Or we see a world in which the earth is healthy and the water and air are clean. We see a world in which all nations live together in peace. We see an America in which the races live in harmony and joy together, and so on. This process gives all participants an opportunity to speak their sacred word, and thus exercise their spiritual power to recreate the world. People's hearts long to create the good, the true, and the beautiful, and we grieve our lost capacity to do so.

Words spoken in normal speech do not necessarily carry spiritual power, but words spoken in sacred process, coming out of silence and heart-felt dedication to the common good, carry moral weight and psychological momentum for both the speaker and the listener. They are words "spoken in faith," and are thus, if loving, accompanied by divine authority.

Seven principles guide our spiritual/political practice:

1. The powers within us—mind and spirit—are greater than all powers outside.
2. Forgiveness and love are both our goal for the world *and* our means of achieving that goal.
3. We do not look away from the problems of the world, for that is negative denial. Rather, we look toward them and pray to be agents of positive change.
4. We embrace both the love and the sorrows of the world, for what is embraced with love is automatically delivered to realms of more positive unfoldment.
5. We will take constructive political action, in accordance with the magnificent opportunities afforded us as citizens of a democratic society. But we do not act in order to oppose what is; we act in order to make another, more positive choice for the future.
6. We seek peace within ourselves at all times, for lack of peace in us will be reflected outside ourselves.
7. We see citizenship as a divine gift, to be used in love's service, for the creation of better, more just, more compassionate world.

ALL around America today, a spontaneous movement is arising, centered around the power of people joining in circles. Wisdom Circles, Womens' Circles, Sacred Circles, and so on—the circle itself is ritualistic tool, uniting inner and outer energies in a very powerful way.

The Citizen Circle is a similar phenomenon, creating a mystical grid of new political possibility around the United States and the world. They help to ground the new political energy.

The key to a successful Citizen Circle is that we speak from the heart about subjects that matter. The agenda includes:

1. Silent meditation or nondenominational devotion.
2. Discussion or visualization of what we as individuals would wish America, or the world, to be like.
3. An educational element such as group reading and discussion. If the meeting is weekly, perhaps one member of the group brings in an article or chapter of a book for group discussion.
4. Citizen lobbying. With every article or discussion, the group should then plan a specific lobbying action, such as letters to an elected official. Remember, we do not all have to be lobbying for the same things or expressing the same opinions.
5. Part of the value of these meetings is that they provide a chance to hear the views of those whom we know are just as intelligent as we, but see things from a different political perspective. If splinter groups grow out of that, whereby we lobby for common things, that is fine and good. But listening to other people's viewpoints keeps our own from calcifying.

Many people open their Circles with prayer, such as the following one:

> Dear God,
> We come together,
> different perspectives,
> different politics,
> different cultures,
> to ask that you heal our country.
> We surrender to you
> the thoughts and attitudes we now hold,
> and empty our minds that they might
> be filled by You.
> Show us to each other,

as You would have us see each other.
Show us the world,
as You would have us see the world.
Guide our listening,
as You would have us hear each other.
Teach us, and inspire us.
Use us on Your behalf.
Amen

In an environment where prayer is either inappropriate or perceived as threatening to some members of the group, a generalized reference to "the spirit of goodness within all of us" or "the love [or light] within our minds" carries with it the power to bring groups of people into spiritual alignment with each other and a higher power.

Martin Luther King, Jr., said, "I am convinced that the universe is under the control of a loving purpose and that in the struggle for righteousness man has cosmic companionship. Behind the harsh appearance of the world there is a benign power. To say God is personal is not to make Him an object among other objects or attribute to Him the finiteness and limitations of human personality; it is to take what is finest and noblest in our consciousness and affirm its perfect existence in Him."

The greatest power is neither money nor technological device; the greatest power is the power of consciousness. So it is that a new politics centers around the arousal of that power, using prayer and meditation to create a forcefield of transformation.

The following are some suggestions for the kinds of prayers that break up old political thought patterns:

1. Pray for every one of the fifty states.
2. Pray for help in giving up judgment toward whatever person in public life, or group of people, you tend to judge.

———

3. Pray for the children of America.

4. Pray for the leaders of America.

5. Pray for the poor in America.

6. Pray for America's criminal population.

7. Pray for all drug addicts and alcoholics.

8. Pray for America's sick.

9. Pray for America's relationship with all other nations.

10. Pray for atonement and amends toward those who have been wronged by us as a nation.

11. Pray for racial healing. Atone for the systemic racism that permeates our social policies today, even if you personally don't consider yourself a racist.

12. Pray for parents and children in America.

13. Pray for husbands and wives in America.

14. Pray for all lovers and friends.

15. Pray for America's environment.

16. Pray for the American economy.

17. Pray for American education.

18. Pray for American health care.

19. Pray for America's homeless.

20. Pray that you might become a better American citizen.

The following are some prayers that might assist your efforts:

> Dear God,
> There was born on this land
> a possibility of freedom
> more expansive than the world had ever known.
>   And the promise still exists.
> There is freedom here
> for some,
> dear Lord,
> but clearly not for all.
>   And the promise still exists.

Help us, Lord,
to free our country from the chains
of our hardened hearts.
    And the promise still exists.
Amen

———

Dear God,
Please bless our children,
and the children of the world.
    May their innocence remain.
Dear God,
Please bless their tender souls.
Lead them away from harsh stimulation
and the violent ways which hurt them.
Cast out of us the things which offend
the spirit of love
in all of us.
Make our children free of all the darkened things in life,
and make us free as well,
dear Lord.
Make us free as well.
In these United States
And in the world,
May only love remain.
Amen

———

Dear God,
We are
the richest nation,
the most blessed of places,
We praise you, Lord, and thank you.
Surely the bounty You have given us
is meant by You to bless the world,

———

Please show us how,
dear God.
Please recreate our culture,
renew our tired lives.
Let light and love
flow down on us,
our country
and our world.
Amen

——

Dear God,
We bless the souls of those who founded these United
States, of all who came before us,
and who struggle still today,
to bring forth all the greatness
and the glory
of America.
Thank you, God,
and them.
Amen

——

Dear God,
Please bless the people of America,
and all people throughout the world.
Use me, God,
in whatever way
You would have me serve.
Show me how to live my life
in such a way as to spread the love
which feeds and redeems us all.
Amen

——

——

Dear God,
May the angels
of America
burst forth across this land,
healing hearts and
blessing souls.
May they awaken yet
the cry of freedom
in one and all,
Release us from bondage,
release us from fear.
Amen

———

Dear God,
Turn back the fist
that sits upon the process of our furtherance,
limiting our good.
Remove it from our hearts,
remove it from our streets,
remove it from our government,
remove it from our land.
Thank you, God.
Amen

———

Dear God,
Please forgive this country
for the racism,
past and present,
which so hides Your light.
Take from us any thoughts we hold,
or feelings we have,
which make firm the darkness.

———

Please show us how to create anew
American society,
that truly we might be as brothers.
Thank you very much,
Amen

—

Dear God,
We don't even know
all the things which are wrong in this country,
but You do,
dear Lord,
You do.
Please reveal to us
what You would have revealed,
and take from us what You would take.
Thank you, God.
Amen

—

Dear God,
May we not be slaves to money.
May our hearts serve higher things.
May money flow into us
abundantly and freely,
according to Your will,
and may it serve Your purpose.
Show us how to hold it in the light.
Amen

—

Dear God,
May our essential nature
as a country
and a people,

awaken on this day.
May the glorious possibilities
of our miraculous beginnings
once more enchant our hearts and
set us free
Of limitation.
Break the chain
of dominance
which false power holds upon us still.
Renew the spirit
of freedom and love
Which are Your truth within us.
Amen

—

Dear God,
Please help us change America,
from a land of violence
to a land of love.
Where there is separation,
please bring union.
Where there is distrust and pain,
please bring reconciliation of our hearts
with each other,
and with You.
May all be blessed
and prosper,
here and throughout the world.
And so it is.
Amen

—

Dear God,
Lead us
where You would have us go,
Show us

—

what You would have us do.
Guide us
in what You would have us say,
and to whom,
that we might serve You best.
Give us hope
that there is yet
another way.
We are open,
we are willing,
we are waiting for Your hand
upon our shoulders and our hearts.
May Your will still yet be done on earth,
as it is in Heaven,
Amen

Dear God,
Please give every mother's child
enough to eat,
in America
and elsewhere.
Give every mother's child
good work to do,
and the strength to do it,
in America and everywhere.
Give every mother's child
the wisdom to see,
and the courage to act,
and the heart to forbear,
in America and everywhere.
Use us to help You, Lord,
to make these things so.
Amen

—

Dear God,
Please forgive us
for how we offend Your spirit,
ignoring the poor,
yet feeding the rich,
not fostering peace,
yet making fortunes
on the instruments of war.
Please turn us around, dear God,
and heal our minds
and hearts.
Please open our eyes,
transform our minds,
that they might be of You,
and You only.
Amen

—

Dear God,
I know not where to go,
but You do.
I know not what to do,
but You do.
I know not how to be,
but You do,
to change this world,
to heal this country.
Please show me, Lord,
For I would do my part.
Amen

—

Dear God,
Please bless our Congress,
our President,
our judges,
and elected officials,
and the people of the United States,
with wisdom
and light
and love
Please bless those who have no voice,
and lend them mine.
Amen

———

Dear God,
There are those
who have too little hope.
There are those who try,
yet feel their dreams
shot down.
There are those who love,
yet feel forgotten
in the madness and the crowds.
Please help them all.
Open wide our hearts
and eyes
and ears,
that we might know and hear each other,
in our joy
and in our pain.
Amen

SOCIAL change will now grow along a vertical axis more than a horizontal one. A few people joined together and thinking deeply will do more to affect the conditions of the world than millions of people joined in superficial thought. That is because the morphic resonance of loving thought is a literal forcefield, not just a metaphorical concept. It is the *sahimsa* of which Gandhi spoke, carrying within itself more potential power than any nuclear bomb or military force. The question is not whether this power exists, or even whether enough people believe that it exists; the question for our time is whether enough of us are prepared to *harness* that power for the purpose of national and planetary healing. Citizen Circles are one way to do that. To speak of love is one thing; to sit in silence with others, to pray, to speak from our hearts, to envision a loving future, to forgive ourselves and each other—these are something else altogether. They are the tools of nonviolence and the seeds of a brand new world.

Some of our most important issues cannot be adequately addressed by merely an intellectual approach to problems. We know this as individuals, but we are just in the beginning stages of applying this understanding to national and international affairs.

As I drove past a Planned Parenthood clinic in a central California town, I noticed that on the one side of the driveway were protesters with picket signs, while on the other side of the driveway was a woman wearing a bulletproof vest, on top of which was written "Clinic." I was stunned at the sight of such a thing, here in America. I almost cried when I saw how far we have descended from our Founders' vision of a creatively deliberative group of people.

People who are free to debate their views but define that debate as screaming at each other, people who are free to express their opinions but dishonor the opinions of others, are not practicing democracy but are in the process of destroying it. Our forefathers foresaw for us a deliberative, consensus-building, reasonable form of political debate. But a generation for whom after-dinner conversation has been replaced on a mass level by after-dinner television has difficulty developing the social maturity necessary for the authentic practice of democracy. Such practice demands our capacity to speak from our depths and listen from our depths. Cultural cacophany is an enemy of democracy.

A challenge of our time is to create an alternative political culture. If our goal is to do that, then it's not just the content of our political conclusions but also the process by which we derive at them that need to be addressed.

I was once giving a lecture to a large audience when the subject of abortion came up in the discussion period of the program. Tensions began to surface; a rip in the emotional fabric of the room was obvious to everyone. One choice was to go for a false positivism, pretending we're all so "spiritual" here that we don't have to delve into issues like that. Such a choice is not transcendence but denial, healing nothing and no one. Another choice was to open the discussion—go for it and see what happens. A third choice offered a different way. I asked the people in the room to close their eyes and silently remain that way for two minutes. I asked that we look within ourselves and call on the spirit of goodness that resides there. I suggested we ask the soul for its wisdom regarding this issue, surrendering our perceptions into the hands of God.

After our two minutes of silence, we resumed conversation. Everyone in the room was quieter, more accepting and compassionate toward the views of others, and more eloquent in stating their own views. What came forward, then, was not so much anyone's particular opinions but everyone's capacity to communicate more deeply. People were truly *heard* that night by people who had previously dismissed their views out of hand. The "right answer" is not a particular view on policy, so much as an experience of each other in which the process of meaningful communication is restored.

We don't need to extend democracy out into the world, so much as to deepen it within ourselves. The day after that lecture, someone who was there remarked to me, "I felt like last night I had an intimate living room conversation regarding abortion with two thousand people." From that intimacy did come healing, and from that kind of healing will come a new America.

BETWEEN a public education system that can hardly be credited with stimulating critical thought and television programming that absolutely destroys it, we are left a dumbed-down culture, ever ready to fight each other but almost incapable of higher debate. Higher questions go right by us, and that is an inestimable loss for any culture. Only when we put the deeper questions on the table can we hope to arrive at deeper answers. Questioning can be messy, but that is how it should be.

Too many times in America today the social maxim among us is, "Let's not talk about religion or politics." Boy, does that leave *me* out at dinner! We don't need to talk less in America; we need to talk more, and more deeply, about things that matter most. And we need to act on what we know, to develop the habit of participating in the democratic process at a much higher level than whining, kvetching, or even just voting.

One night at one of my lectures in New York City, we did the Citizen Circle process of declaring the America we would like to see. Scores of people were proclaiming, "I see an America in which...." After doing the exercise, I went off the stage for a twenty-minute intermission.

When I returned, it was time for a different part of my presentation: responding to questions handed in from members of the audience. I had been doing this format—lecture, intermission, then questions and answers—for years, yet this night was different. Almost every time I read a question, before I could even say anything in response, someone in the audience would speak up! Not raise a hand, but just blurt out an answer—and always a good one. Something significant had occurred here: from merely participating in that exercise, people had subtly shifted from passive to active, from nonparticipatory to participatory, from a mode where "someone else has the answers" to one where "I have the answers." People hadn't *become* wise that night, of course, but many had come closer to *owning* their wisdom that night.

Within minutes, people were talking—completely unprompted by me—of which companies produce their products in countries where child labor is used; the tenets of socially responsible investing; how to include infant and child care in a corporate environment; economic injustice and the U.S. tax code; the dangers of genetically engineered food. It was like tired flowers that had finally been put in water: people are so hungry to participate in something bigger than ourselves, after years of pouring our energies into merely self-centered molds. There *is* such a thing as group intelligence and group conscience, and democracy cannot live without it. Average citizens joined in a dignified environment of deliberation and consensus building—not back rooms where corporate lobbyists and lawyers get to call most of the shots—*that* is the engine that should drive America.

Our collective cynicism and citizen fatigue is the biggest obstacle to breaking democracy's free fall. Some say they don't participate more because there doesn't seem to be any one issue to rally around like there was in the sixties, some say they feel hopeless and that it doesn't matter what you do or who you vote for anyway, some say that money has it all sewn up, and so on. But in reality, money—as powerful as it is—doesn't actually vote. Power has been grabbed *from* the people, but it has also been abdicated *by* the people, and we should take responsibility for that.

There seems to be no issue to rally around only because there is no one *single* issue. There are many to rally around, in fact, and people in this country deeply care about our collective problems. Most of us have chosen not to participate in solving them politically, only because we haven't thought that politics was an effective way to do that. But politics is not a rigid institution. In truth, it will be anything we choose it to be, and as in every other area of American life today, people are making brand-new choices.

A new politics is emerging for the twenty-first century, defining power not by dominance but by sharing. We don't need the traditional political establishment to say, "Oh wow, what a powerful idea." They'll see this later, which is how it always works. When complementary medicine burst on the scene, no one asked the AMA's permission! Medical physicians made fun of metaphysicians, as we held support groups, prayed for patients, stressed forgiveness, and so on. But it's a whole new world now—our most prestigious medical institutions are acknowledging the "psycho-immunological factor," the effects of spirituality and consciousness in healing the physical body—and former cynics are not laughing anymore.

So, of course, traditional political types will laugh at a metapolitical emphasis where love, atonement, peace, and reverance for life are seen as dominant political values. That's okay; they won't laugh forever. Politicians, like medical doctors, aren't demi-gods anymore. They're our *partners* in healing society. What we need in America now is not so much a visionary leader or a visionary media; what we need is a visionary constituency, and that is what is forming. Organizations and projects are popping up all over the country, helping to build that constituency, giving us a framework for meaningful silence, meaningful discussion, and meaningful political action.

Inner activism meets outer activism: Voilà! Holistic politics.

8

CITIZEN
POWER

SEVERAL years ago, I made my first congressional constituent call. It was an initiation of sorts into citizen power.

The U.S. Senate was debating at that time—and then turned down—an amendment to the budget bill that would have added a 43-cent tobacco tax on every pack of cigarettes, creating $30 billion in revenue to pay for health insurance for millions of children of the working poor. The amendment, which lost by only ten votes, had been proposed by conservative Republican Senator Orrin Hatch of Utah and liberal Democratic Senator Edward Kennedy of Massachusetts.

President Clinton had helped defeat the amendment because Republican Majority Leader Trent Lott had called it a "deal breaker" in working out the budget agreement. Opponents of the amendment were saying amazing things like, "Voting for this bill will actually hurt the poor because they'll just keep on smoking but it will be more expensive."

Senator Hatch said, "It's Joey versus Joe Camel, and no procedural niceties can obscure this reality and everybody here knows it." Senator Kennedy said, "We shall offer it again and again until we prevail. It's more important to protect children than to protect the tobacco industry."

I saw in the newspaper that one of my Senators voted to defeat the rider. She's a good Senator and I respect her, particularly her stand on gun control, but on this one issue I strongly disagreed with her vote. I called the main switchboard at the Capitol in Washington, D.C. (202-224-3121; that number should be written down and put on the refrigerator door of every home in the United States), and asked for her office. The switchboard connects you immediately to whatever office you request.

"Senator Feinstein's office." A nice young staffer was on the other end of the line.

"Hello," I said. "This is a constituent call. My name is Marianne Williamson, and I'm calling to express profound disappointment that the Senator helped defeat the rider yesterday that would have provided money for children's health insurance. Could you explain to me why she did that please?"

"Certainly," he said, and put me on hold. In a few seconds he was back. "The Senator felt she had to do it because the Majority Leader said it was a deal breaker for the budget deal."

"Yes, I know that he said that. I read that in the paper. But quite a few people argued that that was a bluff. Why must we so consistently cave in to those who would have us balance the budget on the backs of our children, rather than on the back of the tobacco industry? Could you explain that to me, please?"

"Yes, certainly," he said, and put me on hold again.

In a few moments, he returned. "I was told to tell you that the President himself called here yesterday, and asked that the Senator vote the way she did."

"Would you please tell the Senator that my response to that is, 'So?'"

"Yes, of course," he said.

"Please tell the Senator that at least one of her constituents wants to go on record saying that doing the right thing is never a wrong move."

"Thank you," he said, "I will tell her that."

Like hell he will, I thought, as I put down the phone. I had no illusions, of course, that the Senator would be told what I said. But I knew this: if she received a hundred calls like that—or, better yet, two hundred—she sure *would* hear about it, and I even think she would care. These people still run for election.

There are millions of people in America who read about what happens in Washington and are disgusted at how we keep selling out to various industries at the expense of the American families, day after day. But too many of us don't call Washington and don't write any letters; we just feel the darkness in our guts, knowing what we know but doing nothing. It's like David saying about Goliath, "Geez, he really is big. Maybe I won't do this."

But Goliath isn't *that* big. Things aren't *that* bad in America. And each of us has a slingshot.

Paradoxically, part of the problem with an overly yang culture is that it produces overly yin personalities. Without the yin of peace and serenity, there is no character formation; without that, there is no capacity for the yang of powerful personal action. We desperately need both. There is no machine, technology, or scientific project that can renew and restore democracy. If we want that done, it's a job we have to do ourselves.

AFTER he left the Presidency, Harry Truman was asked how it felt no longer being President. He responded that he had gotten promoted to a better job: "Mr. Citizen."

Most Americans do not even vote, feeling politics is like a fading reality having little to do with their actual lives. In many ways they are right. It is a spectator sport now, when it was intended to be a participatory drama. No American citizen should be watching the action from the sidelines; each of us has lines to say.

And to say that I vote and therefore participate fully as a citizen is like saying that I pay child support and therefore I'm a real parent.

"The people of every country are the only safe guardians of their own rights," wrote Thomas Jefferson, "and are the only instruments which can be used for their destruction. It is an axiom in my mind that our liberty can never be safe but in the hands of the people themselves. . . ."

Many Americans do not exercise their rights because they have come to take them for granted or underestimate their power. It is often when people have been denied their civil rights that they most appreciate how important such rights are.

Michele McDonald, an African-American single mother who lives in the inner city of Hartford, Connecticut, said regarding the President's Summit on Volunteerism, held in Philadelphia in 1997,

The Conference is a nice concept, but it's missing the element of real democracy. What we want are the tools of power. We want to be the driving force of the richness of our own community.

We want to be the ones to determine the needs of our own community; we appreciate people coming in to help, but we don't want to just be an object of someone's "needs assessment" program. That makes us victims, and it disempowers us. What we want is to learn the tools of democracy, so we're not just drowning in the system—we want to learn *Civics*!

The system shouldn't be deciding what I need; I want to tell them what I need. I want to learn how to be a better citizen in my community and my nation. I want to help my neighbors be more focused on their gifts than on their deficits. What I want to know is how to empower my own community, so we've got real input on where we're going. We want to be empowered to take care of our own neighborhood.

Those people don't want us to have the tools because then we'd have real power. That's what's really going on.

Sometimes they say they want parents from the community to

sit on their boards and things, but once we get there, they don't want us to know how to really use the system. We're supposed to just sit there and be quiet, but they can point to us and say, "See, they're included."

This woman understands the game that's being played here: a system that constitutionally owes her much is patting itself on the back for giving her just a little. Michele is part of a burgeoning impulse to take back the tools of democracy. We take them back by using them.

Even Michele's nine-year-old daughter, Giavanna, has gotten into the act. She took part in an essay-writing contest sponsored by the local police department. Giavanna won first prize—a new bicycle—with an essay entitled "How a Bill Becomes a Law." The bill that she and her classmates worked on was titled "Having Ice Cream Every Day for Lunch."

What neither the Democrats nor the Republicans have emphasized is how to empower Americans as citizens. John Perkins, leader of the Christian Community Development Association, has said, "It's not enough to give someone a fish, or even to teach them how to fish. Now we have to ask who owns the pond."

WHILE the American political system should be a context for the discovery of solutions, the system itself is beset by some of our most severe wounds. The selfishness, violence, absence of teamwork, shortage of creative thinking, lack of courage to take risks, propensity to put the protection of entrenched interests before the pursuit of truth, obsolete hierarchical management systems, glorification of external resources, underemphasis on internal resources, lack of integrity, and diminished standards of excellence that are all hallmarks of a crumbling system are, if anything, more prevalent in politics than in any other institution in America. A weakened structure cannot give us strength. Far from being a fount of answers, politics in America is a big part of our problem. If democracy is a river that would provide the water to help us spring back to life, current politics is a dam that holds the water back. It is a conversation stuck at the level of a shouting match, an adversarial us-versus-them debate of total polarization and very little synergy.

Instead of endeavoring to present the political issues of our time in as historically and socially significant ways as possible to ensure the deepest exercise of democracy, the political establishment has turned itself into a clone of the advertising industry and the workhorse of a ruling class. It works less to serve than to exploit us, to manipulate the electorate for the sake of its own power.

Neither Democrats nor Republicans seem to see the writing on the wall; perhaps it is still written in invisible ink. But it is bold and in caps nonetheless: our political parties have abdicated the sacred trust we placed in them and we are married to them in our minds no longer. Their eviction notice has already been signed, though they seem not yet to have received it. We have emotionally pulled away. It is a mistake to think our lack of expressed anger at the consistency of sordid government dealings and the obvious selling out of the average American's greater good means we're not interested or that we do not care. What we feel, in fact, is more potent than anger; we feel the kind of detached disgust that is significant because it isn't angry. We're not even interested in struggling with them anymore. That's when you know that a marriage is over.

Political parties at their best stand for something: ideas about what the country should be, ideas about how to achieve that, and ways for the average citizen to be involved in the effort. The average American citizen today can feel that we are mainly seen by the major parties as mere cannon fodder in their fights with each other over the prizes of office. When parties are what they should be, people are legitimately willing to commit their loyalty. Today, this is less and less true.

Our political energy is up for grabs, or for reinvention. The largest voting block in America is Independent, and it's growing. Jesse Ventura was just the beginning. We are open to the possibility that there might be a better way.

In his Farewell Address, George Washington had the following to say regarding political parties:

> They serve to organize faction, to give it an artificial and extraordinary force; to put in the place of the delegated will of the Nation, the will of a party; often a small but artful and enterprising minority of the Community; and, according to the alternate triumphs of different parties, to make the public administration the Mirror of the ill concerted and incongruous projects of faction, rather than the organ of consistent and wholesome plans digested by common counsels and modified by mutual interests. However combinations or Associations of the above description may now and then answer popular ends, they are likely, in the course of time and things, to become potent engines, by which cunning, ambitious and unprincipled men will be enabled to subvert the Power of the People, and to usurp for themselves the reins of Government; destroying afterwards the very engines which have lifted them to unjust dominion.

He added, "Let me now ... warn you in the most solemn manner against the baneful effects of the spirit of party."

The failure of American politics to engage us fully is not an inherent weakness in the American system of government, but only in the entrenched political establishment that would have us believe we have no alternative to them. There's nothing in the Constitution that says, "You will be divided into two main political parties, Democrats and Republicans, and together they will determine the direction of the country, even if that direction is into the ground." Their shared dominance of our political system is merely a product of our own malaise. They're so big for no other reason than we've all played so small.

The Democratic-Republican machinery dominates American politics, and the media act like their puppets. God forbid Americans should get to seriously hear what various third-party candidates actually have to say. During the 1996 Presidential elections, the Debate Commission (who *are* these guys? Former Democratic and Republican operatives, of course) determined that only Clinton and Dole could participate in the debates because they were the only *serious* candidates. I love this; isn't this what they used to do in the Communist world—determine people's choices for them? Capitalism keeps us so busy with a variety of choices concerning the things we buy that we don't stop to ask ourselves why it is that we get so little to choose from in politics.

During the 1996 Presidential election, there was no serious debate regarding race, poverty, the economic gap between rich and poor, environmental issues, or the welfare of America's children. Why? The candidates didn't have to go there. Nothing demanded it. There's basically no competition!

Most Americans would be very surprised if they knew the extent to which third parties have been denied full access to our political process, particularly over the last thirty years. While historically, third parties have been a very important contribution to American democracy, bringing to the political table such issues as abolition, women's right to vote, antimonopoly legislation, child labor laws, and even Social Security, slowly, ever since the late 1880s, both Democratic and Republican legislatures have passed laws making it more and more difficult for third-party candidates to get on ballots around the country.

The healthiest period of our democratic system was from the 1870s to the 1880s, when voter turnout was around 80 percent. During that time, many powerful third parties existed, keeping the vast majority of voters engaged in the political process owing to a genuine sense of viable political alternatives. Before 1888, there were no ballot access requirements; from 1888 to 1920, minimal requirements were passed; during the 1930s, ballot access laws became far more restrictive; and in the 1960s, laws began to be passed making third-party involvement in the electoral process extremely difficult. It has been noted that our great-great-grandfathers, if they were American voters, had a greater opportunity to change public policy with their votes than we do today.

The United States has become the most discriminatory democracy in the world, since most democracies treat all parties the same and have minimal ballot access requirements, if any. Since 1998, if a new party wants to truly participate in America's election process, it must collect *5 million* valid signatures. Meanwhile, Democratic and Republican candidates need submit no signatures at all. Abraham Lincoln became President on the platform of a party that had been in existence for only six years at that time; one can hardly even imagine such a thing happening today. "Active and vigorous third parties play a vital role in maintaining the health of our two-party system," writes Richard Winger, editor of *Ballot Access News.* Without their involvement, the system calcifies, for the two main parties know that there is no serious alternative to *them.* Every day, and every election, the average American voter feels less and less power to affect true change in U.S. policy. It feels like our elections are becoming expensive stage shows, little more than entertainment extravaganzas. Until we demand that third parties have more access to the process, this will only get worse instead of better.

I heard quite a few people speaking on television before the last Presidential election, bemoaning the choice between Clinton and Dole, unhappy that neither candidate represented their highest hopes. And yet most Americans, even if there is a third-party candidate who more nearly expresses their views, are afraid to vote for that person lest the Democrat or Republican who most offends them might then win. This makes logical sense, but not quantum sense. Democracy should mean that we are cowed by nothing and no one. We need to retrieve our capacity to say, "This is what *I* think." And we need to support the political candidates who think the way we do, and have the courage to say so.

THERE are so many talented people in America, with so many brilliant, heartfelt ideas and projects that improve the lot of human beings in every corner of our society. Yet their talents are vastly underused, even obstructed by the current status quo. What these thinkers and practitioners offer, while desperately needed by society at large, is often of little use to our current political system. Their ideas do not necessarily make money or solidify political power; what their ideas do is serve the people.

We must concoct something new now: If we harness our best ideas, our love for each other, and our commitment to the furtherance and betterment of our society, then a new vortex of social and political power will emerge in our midst. It seems to some as though this is just a pipe dream, but the most serious among us would not think that at all. In a cosmic sense, money is not serious. In a cosmic sense, business is not serious. In a cosmic sense, the game of politics is not serious.

But love is very serious indeed.

IF we were serious about democracy, voter registration would occur automatically on an American citizen's eighteenth birthday, voting would be held on a Saturday or Sunday and possibly for more than one day, and the polls would be open for twenty-four hours. It cannot be said that the current system *encourages* voter participation.

If we were serious about democracy, we would mandate free TV time for all candidates, where *they* are free to speak for themselves but their Madison Avenue handlers have to keep their paws off our brains. Our political candidates should not be sold like soda pop.

If we were serious about democracy, our legislators would not feel free to continuously avoid grappling with the challenge of limiting the influence of money on the electoral system. Americans have turned off politics now because they know it's all just become a game. What we need to remember, however, is that while current politics *is* just a game, democracy is not. It's as though we own a house and we do not like the current tenants. You don't avoid the house or burn down the house; you remove the tenants. *N'est-ce pas?*

While our party affiliations come and go, our citizenship itself is a permanent aspect of our relationship to this country. And citizenship *is* a relationship. It is, when we allow it to be, a process of interaction that fosters growth and betterment on both sides. America is better off when we're involved with its governance, and we ourselves are better off when we can effectively participate in making the world a better place.

Below are some very simple basics for making a political difference. Sometimes something very small can go a long way, and if all of us did even a few of these things, this country would completely change.

GETTING INFORMATION ON BECOMING INVOLVED

There are many avenues through which one can find out what is happening on a daily, weekly, or monthly basis in our government, both on Capitol Hill and at the White House, and at the state and city levels.

Cable television seems to launch a new all-news channel as often as they break a story. C-Span and C-Span 2 show live coverage of Congress when it's in session, important political speeches and panels, as well as programs with viewer call-in segments.

One of the easiest ways to become informed is to read the newspaper. It's true that you don't want to overdose on this, but a daily scan of one major paper, particularly the op-ed page, keeps you generally well informed. Most major newspapers are now available on the World Wide Web, as well. Most important, don't forget alternative press like the *Utne Reader*.

WRITING TO ELECTED OFFICIALS

It is estimated that fewer than 10 percent of the voters will ever write to elected officials. Yet *contacting our elected officials with a letter is an important part of making a difference.* They *work for you.* They theoretically want to hear our views, and they definitely can't afford to ignore them. It's our responsibility to express those views.

Like voting, communicating our views in the political arena metaphysically increases our own power. The universe registers our every serious intention and vigorous action on behalf of what we perceive to be a greater good.

You may think your elected officials are flooded with letters on issues you care about. The truth is that most members of Congress receive fewer than a hundred letters on any one issue. On the state level, elected officials often receive fewer than ten letters on a particular issue. Your letter can carry a lot of weight.

Your opinions are particularly important when an issue is timely—for example, when a vote is expected or when there is a lot of news coverage of the subject.

Tips for your letter: Be brief, address only one issue at a time, keep the letter down to four or five sentences; say why the issue or legislation matters to you; state your reason for opposing or supporting a particular bill. If you have particular expertise, then say what it is. Be positive and constructive, give compliments if they're sincere. Send a copy to your local newspaper to help build support for the issue. Use the appropriate title of the elected official. (Note: A country music star's mother once met Al Gore and asked him, "And what do you do?" When told he was the Vice-President, she said, "Of what record company?" It couldn't have gone over well.) After you have written once, then keep up the contact and periodically communicate that you're following closely what happens; thank the official and state that you'll be following up with a phone call in a week to receive a response, and then do so.

As effective as one letter is, twenty-five on the same issue are even better. Getting others who are concerned about the same issue to send letters is not as hard as you might think. Use a Citizen Circle; write letters together.

KNOW YOUR REPRESENTATIVE

On the Web, www.vote-smart.org/congress/congress.html is a government-run Web site that allows us to find our representatives in Congress by entering by zip code.

—

Send your letter to:

The Honorable _____
United States Senate
Washington, D.C. 20510

The Honorable _____
United States House of Representatives
Washington, D.C. 20515

Or you can go straight to the source via computer. Both the legislative and executive branches have Web pages: www.House.gov, www.Senate.gov, and www.WhiteHouse.gov.

DON'T HESITATE TO PICK UP THE PHONE

By phone, you can call the Capitol Switchboard at 202-224-3121. The switchboard can connect you with your Representative's or Senator's office. The White House Switchboard is 202-456-1414, and the White House Comments Line is 202-456-1111.

Say who you are, why you're calling, give facts and background about the issue, state your position and why, say what you want, and use a pleasant but firm closing that lets them know you'll be contacting them further. Make sure you follow up with a letter.

My experience calling Senator Feinstein's office made it clear to me that such calls are expected, and they are almost always treated with respect.

WRITING FOR THE OP-ED PAGE

This is easier than you might think. If you have a strong idea or opinion about a public issue that you'd like to express, write it out. Write it well, communicating your personal experiences. Make your position clear from the beginning, get right to the subject, make your sentences relatively short. Be sure all names are correct and all quotations accurate. End your article with a forceful conclusion, and write your name, address, and phone numbers on your submission. A good op-ed piece is about 750 words, or three double-spaced typewritten pages. Write in the active voice, get your facts right, and make sure you're adding some new insight into the argument.

MEETING WITH ELECTED OFFICIALS

Visiting elected officials is an important part of promoting our points of view. A citizen visiting his or her elected officials is visibly identifying himself or herself as a constituent or a voter. Because the official is focusing on you as an individual and as a voter, a visit will have great impact.

One of the important ways of affecting change with elected officials is by building a strong relationship. Developing strong relationships with them is an important part of exercising our power in a democracy. It is especially important to develop relationships with staffs of elected officials. Elected officials and their staffs are eager to get information that they can use in speeches and when working with constituents.

1. Make an appointment by calling the elected official.
2. Indicate the issues you want to discuss.
3. Study the issues to be covered in the visit. Keep the discussion to one or perhaps two issues.
4. Keep the atmosphere friendly and open. You are there to exchange ideas; under no circumstances should you become angry.
5. Limit the time of the meeting. Don't let the conversation drag.
6. If you don't know the answer to a question the official asks you, just say so and explain that you'll get the information. Make sure you follow through.

7. Leave some information with the elected official on the issue. This will help him or her remember your visit.

8. Follow your visit with a thank-you note. Remember—your main objective is to establish a continuing dialogue with your elected officials.

There is a wonderful Web site that is a kind of all-purpose citizen activism guide. At the Project Vote Smart Web page, www.vote-smart.org, entering your zip code will tell you not only who your elected officials are and their addresses but also everything from their voting records to their biographies to their main funding sources.

If you're online, this is a wonderful opportunity to learn how to express yourself and participate powerfully in the process.

For more information about Citizen Circles and the work of the Global Renaissance Alliance around the country and the world, call 1-800-299-7573. Or go to www.renaissancealliance.org, on the Web. In our joining with others lies all the strength we need.

SITTING around waiting for someone to tell us what to do is not the pulse of the moment or in keeping with the gift of democracy. The zeitgeist is to do the thing that each of us knows is the one pure thing that stands before us on the road of life, the undone task of personal growth or community involvement that paves the way to our higher becoming. That is the critical issue in democracy today: that each of us rises to the nobler places within us, to the stuff of integrity, excellence, and love.

No one can lift the fog in your mind except you, yourself. Some of us need to read more; some of us need to pray more; some of us need to go to therapy; some of us need to get a job; some of us need to be more generous; some of us need to participate more fully in our family or community; some of us need to forgive someone, some of us need to ask forgiveness; almost all of us need to become more politically involved. All of us need to do something that we know is the next step in the journey of our soul's unfoldment, and most of us know deep in our hearts what that is.

Leadership itself is changing, from a top-down, old-fashioned Newtonian model of someone acting on a system from the outside to try to change it, to a new-paradigm image of change from within. The primary responsibility of leadership in the era now upon us is to hold a space for the genius of others. In the presence of someone who believes in us, we move more quickly into who we might become. But the major work to be done is still up to each of us.

In the words of Francis Bacon, "Knowledge is power." There are universal laws of consciousness that apply to social change. I think of them as the Rules of Renaissance.

1. It is always our prerogative, as individuals and as nations, to choose again: to say no to a direction we've been moving in and yes to a new one. Our greatest power is our capacity to change our minds.
2. Alignment with higher principle is always supported by invisible forces.
3. If an energy is not in alignment with divine Truth, it is ultimately temporary. It will not last forever and is more vulnerable than it appears.
4. The universe is impersonally invested in evolving toward goodness, and uses any available conduit for purposes of doing so. Willingness to be so used activates the conduit. You're as good for the job as anyone else, and your past is totally irrelevant.
5. Don't expect the old order to like you.

6. A life of love and effort on behalf of the collective good promises the satisfaction of knowing that you are doing what you are born to do. You are not, however, promised specific results as you might define them.

7. Your happiness regarding the reality that's coming is a more potent method of social conversion than is your anger regarding the reality now.

As my father used to say, "You know. Now do."

9

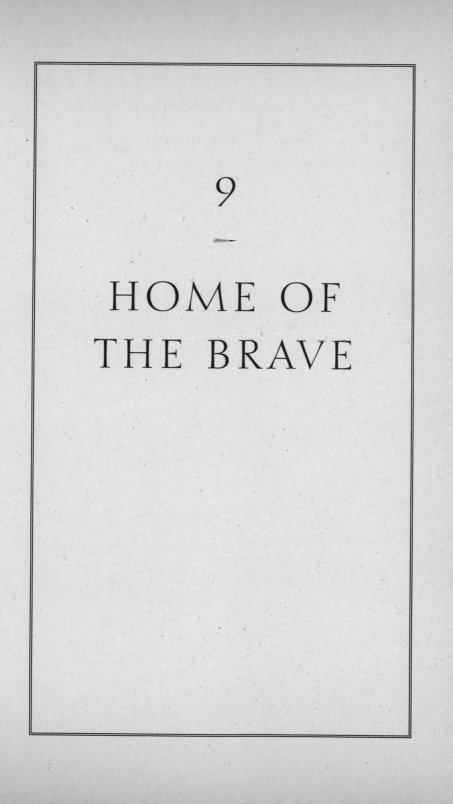

HOME OF
THE BRAVE

How many times we have all sung the song, "America the Beautiful." The line, "And crown thy good with brotherhood," remains poignant thoughout the generations.

I heard the late U.S. Congressman Walter Capps tell the following story. It is a traditional rabbinical tale.

A rabbi was giving instruction to some children, when he posed this question: how do you know the night is over and the day has come? Puzzled, the children took some time to answer. Then one of them ventured, "You know the night is over and the day has come when, at dawn, you look out at a tree, and you can tell whether it is an apple or pear tree." The rabbi acknowledged this response, but repeated the question. A second student offered, "You know the night is over and the day has come when you see an animal in the distance, and you can tell whether it is a donkey or a horse." The rabbi acknowledged this response too, then repeated the question. At this the students, too puzzled to know how to answer, asked the rabbi to solve the dilemma he had posed. The rabbi said, "You know the night is over and the day has come when you look into the eyes of any human being, and you see there your brother or your sister; for, if you do not see your brother or your sister, it is still night—the day hasn't come."

———

And are we, the citizens of this planet earth, brothers—or are we not? That is the fundamental question underlying world events. How we answer that question will make all the difference. If we are not brothers, then it is reasonable to continue to live as we live now. If we are brothers, after all, then information such as the following gives us pause, and makes us question our priorities.

If we could, at this time, shrink the earth's population to a village of precisely one hundred people, with all existing human ratios remaining the same, it would look like this:

- There would be 57 Asians, 21 Europeans, 14 from the Western Hemisphere (North and South), and 8 Africans.
- 70 would be nonwhite, 30 white.
- 70 would be non-Christian, 30 Christian.
- Fifty percent of the entire world's wealth would be in the hands of only 6 people. All 6 would be citizens of the United States.
- 70 would be unable to read.
- 50 would suffer from malnutrition.
- 80 would live in substandard housing.
- Only 1 would have a college education.

When King Hussein of Jordan died in February 1999, leaders from throughout the world went to Amman for his funeral. People who normally do not speak to each other, who spend their lives seeking to destroy each other, who have sent men and women to their deaths in battle against each other, stood side by side and were reminded, for one brief moment at least, that in the end there is only the silence of God.

An awesome assemblage of world power was there, including Presidents and leaders from over fifty countries. President Clinton remarked, "It was really a beautiful sight: people coming from all around the world, countries that are at each other's throats, here meeting in peace and friendship and the sanctity of the umbrella of this great man."

The King, who had dedicated his life to bringing people together, had achieved that goal in death. Not only those who attended the funeral but also millions more throughout the world who watched the rites on television were brought together in reverence and awe before the power of life and death.

Why should it take death to humble us? What is the consciousness that we finally get to, which would save the world if only we would get to it sooner? Why will the leaders of the world unite in tragedy, but not yet in celebration? What can we do to hasten the day when the state of love underlying all things becomes the dominant consciousness of the world?

Funerals can be spiritually unifying events. Perhaps what those world leaders experienced at King Hussein's funeral is a level of simplicity and innocence not unlike a child's. We need to find that simplicity and live there, cleave to that place and pray never to leave. It is our *only safety*. If left to the children, the world would stay innocent. But we have created in America a culture that lures them away from that innocence. Perhaps we should be thinking less how to educate our children than how to protect them from the teachings of our modern world: the teaching that *things* are everything, that money is worth stealing for, that life is cheap, that other people "aren't like us," that somehow suffering doesn't matter, that war is always somewhere else, and that violence is somehow fun.

We try to teach our children to grow up to be leaders, and that is good. But what kinds of leaders? Leaders who exploit great masses of people so that the standard of living of their own people can remain high? Leaders who increase a financial bottom line at the expense of human and natural resources? Leaders who place the welfare of corporations before the welfare of men, women, and children?

Or do we not want to raise our children to rise up in their time, and with their voices mighty, exclaim, "Enough already!" There were leaders in the world who are trying to do that. But we have not yet created a strong enough field of consciousness in the world to form the necessary firmament, the grid of possibility, to turn the human tide from violence to love. In the century ahead of us, if it is to be a century of peace and possibility, leaders of the world will come together as they did at King Hussein's funeral, and pray, as they surely did for him, and wish for peace for the living as well as the dead. At some point in the development of our species, our leaders will turn to each other and experience a common eureka, a common moment of searing vision and electric understanding. They will sit together, in silence and in prayer, and see within them the glorious possibility of a world in which we fight no more, and mothers cry in anguish no more, and children starve by the millions no more, and peace will be ours at last.

When will this occur?

That depends totally on the state of our consciousness. This is very different from saying it depends on the state of our armies, our military, our economies, or our diplomacy. We tend to ask, like Job, "How long, oh God, how long?" But what's really happening is the opposite of that: surely God is asking, "How long, oh children, how long?" How long will *we* wait before the preciousness of all human life is placed higher on our list of values?

We cannot save the world without God's help, and neither can He save the world without ours.

I've led several group tours abroad. It has been one of my most satisfying professional experiences, watching it dawn on a group of Americans that the world outside our borders isn't quite what they had thought. Americans have a unique perspective, inhabiting a very large continent surrounded on two sides by huge oceans. For a long time in our history this provided relative safety from foreign enemies, and independence from the vital concerns of most of the rest of the world. But those days are over. Our fate is now intrinsically tied up with the fate of all humanity, and the destructive weapons that make up the arsenals of the world today would have little trouble making it over the oceans. While we have been warned in recent days of the probability of terrorist attacks on the continental United States some time in the next few years, Americans still act as though we are immune to such things, as though the oceans—and our original allegiance to high and noble principles—still protect us. We have an entrenched perception of separateness, even superiority, regarding the rest of the world. Transforming that consciousness is very important if we are to prepare the way for peace in the century ahead.

There is no greatness in the absence of humility. In the larger scheme of God's universe, the United States is just a little dot on a very little planet. Even our most boastful President, Theodore Roosevelt, knew the value of this enlightened perspective. He used to bring guests at his home, Sagamore Hill, on Long Island, out onto the lawn on a fine, clear summer night and say, "Look, look at the stars." They'd just stand and look for minutes or even hours. Then Roosevelt would flash his famous grin and say, "All right, I think we feel insignificant enough now—let's go to bed."

Our deepest understanding of who we are often stems from seeing ourselves in relation to others. The average American doesn't travel abroad, and this is to our detriment. Americans are propagandized by education and media and self-serving politicians to think that certain things in life are the better way simply because they are *our* way. This places us in almost ridiculous situations vis-à-vis the rest of the world, particularly as we reach the end of the millennium.

Other nations tend to look at us with rolled eyes more than most Americans seem to have any idea. We are a two-hundred-year-old society in the habit of giving lectures about high civilization to people who have been around for hundreds, even thousands of years. Our own homelessness, poverty, violence, and crisis in health care make living in certain other nations look like a day at the beach compared to America, yet we hold forth on how the citizens of those nations could have what we have, if only they would do what we do. We have a higher standard of living in this country, but not necessarily a better standard of living, and everyone except us seems to know this.

The average American is less well read and informed about world events and situations than are our European counterparts, our children are less well educated, we imprison six times more people than any other nation (including Russia and China), and we are the only Western industralized nation that does not have universal health care. We lecture others about human rights (sometimes legitimately), while other nations regard health care as a human right. We go about singing the praises of democracy, but we don't ask ourselves why, if we love it so much, we don't make it easier for people to vote. We talk endlessly about family values in this country, while taking less good care of our children than any other nation with similar resources to do so.

"I am certain," said President Kennedy, "that after the dust of centuries has passed from our cities, we too, will be remembered not for victories or defeats in battle or politics, but for our contribution to the human spirit." I foresee an America in which our contribution to the human spirit is our highest national concern. And when enough of us foresee that, then that is what will come to be. The magnificent gift of who each of us really is, and what we came to earth to give, is awaiting our expression. It will genuinely be the New Order of the Ages proclaimed on our Great

Seal, when America remembers the greatness of her purpose and every American feels they have a part in making it manifest.

Such light will emanate from our shores on that day. The blessings of God will rain down upon us, and through us to the entire world. Our children will know the joy of a deeply peaceful world, and we—wherever we are at that time—will have the knowledge that we helped create it. All of this awaits us on the other side of our current illusions. This is not the time to fall more deeply asleep. This is a time to awaken, to be active, and to be glad. There is a promise that was bequeathed to us, which is ours to hold and then pass on to our children. It is a sacred promise. We are part of the American river of destiny, running through time and carrying with it the extraordinary gift of one great idea: that there can be a land where all are free to be and to become their essential selves. This is more than an inspired idea: it comes straight from the Mind of God. Keeping faith with it is keeping faith with Him, and His help will be with us whenever we do.

WHEN King Saul saw that young David, unskilled in the ways of war, was the only Israelite courageous enough to take on the giant Goliath, he offered him his armor to wear in battle. David put on the king's armor but then removed it. The armor would only slow him down and weigh him down. It would not be armor, but lack of armor, that would empower David in facing Goliath.

Israel's warriors had been taught the ways of war, and yet when the ultimate test came along, they were not brave enough to face it. David, on the other hand, was young, a musician, a shepherd—not a warrior. What looked like his lack of preparation for taking on the force of evil turned out to be simply a different *kind* of preparation—a preparation of the spirit.

David could not imitate what others had done, but he knew to trust himself and his own abilities, to wage battle in another way. And that is what is happening in the world today. There is a new Davidic impulse, a renaissance of hope, and it cannot express itself through the old, tried, world-weary ways. It's not imitating something old but rather creating something new. It is a mystical revolution that will usher in a mystical age.

In some ways, history is something to respect. In other ways, it is something best interrupted. As we enter the new millennium, peace will be forged not only by those who study war but also by those who study peace. The peaceful warrior has an expanded, not a diminished, skill set. Health is much more than the absence of illness; it is the cultivation of health. And peace is much more than the absence of war; it is the cultivation of peace.

From racial healing workshops and youth initiatives in the inner city, to peace-building projects throughout the world, to meditation meetings at military headquarters, there is an emerging global movement toward an alternative mode of peace creation. It is nothing short of an unstoppable force, and every day people are joining the ranks.

I saw a photograph on the front page of a newspaper, showing an American soldier in Bosnia physically keeping apart two women who were having a violent argument. One woman was a Muslim seeking to return to her home and the other was a Serb trying to keep her away. The soldier, one of America's "peacekeepers" in the region, was a valiant referee.

As I looked at that picture, I thought how wonderful it would be if the soldier himself had the tools to actually help these women heal their relationship. The armies and police of our future will include conflict resolution as a part of their training, as in some places they already do. Then we are most prepared to help those in the Middle East; Ireland; Bosnia; East Los Angeles;

Washington, D.C.; and elsewhere find the capacity to move beyond the barriers that divide us so dangerously to the peace that lies beyond.

The fact that the term "peacekeeper" was invented means our society has evolved to the point where we are ready to embrace its meaning. Conflict resolution, nonviolence, and community building are to peace what guns are to war. The full actualization of their potential force, however, remains on the horizon. As a loving critical mass coalesces, as hearts around the world continue to yearn and work for peace, then new forms will emerge to actualize our new planetary vision. This new wine, however, cannot be put in old bottles. The old bottles are inadequate to the task at hand.

Our political establishment tends to respond solely to circumstances; enlightenment responds to vision. Traditional politics is locked into reaction to how things are; with spirit added to the equation, we are free to create something else, to proactively serve a vision of how things could be. The choice is between the human race merely repeating our past, or freeing our future to be something entirely new.

Every morning as I walk my daughter into her school, where innocence and enchantment surround her, I remind myself that on earth today we have the means to make this level of sweetness the material norm for every child. The specifics would vary, of course, because what I want for my child is not what everyone would want for theirs. But my basic dreams—for her safety, her health, her education, her freedom to pursue her own dreams—these I share with all parents everywhere. I am constantly struck by how lucky I am, how lucky she is, and how painful are the lives of so many. There is a lesson here, and a challenge to us all.

A critical mass of people—and while no one can say for sure what constitutes a critical mass, it is thought to be somewhere around 11 percent—meditating on a new vision for the world would tip the planetary field of energy in the direction of peace and justice for all. If enough of us pray for and commit to this peace on a daily basis, holding the vision in sacred silence for at least two minutes, then a miracle will occur. If we imagine a world lit from within, filled with happy people living whatever lives they choose and unburdened by the violence of a world gone mad, then our minds will become conduits through which God Himself can work. Holding the vision of a world in which everyone is *loved* will lift our minds and hearts, make brilliant our thoughts and tender our emotions. The vision itself will cleanse and transform us, making us who we need to be in order to bring it forth. Such is the work of God, through David and through all of us, in Israel of old, in America today, in all the world, throughout all time.

And so it is, and will forever be: love reasserts itself, every morning, every time.

IMAGINE if every member of the United Nations kept one delegate permanently stationed there to spend all day silently blessing every other nation of the world. Imagine humanity committed to universal love, meditating on peace, studied and practiced in the cultural, educational, artistic, philosophical, and diplomatic arts of waging peace. Imagine a world in which war no longer exists. That world is just around the corner, as soon as *we* turn a corner. "More than an end to war, we want an end to the beginnings of all wars," wrote President Franklin Roosevelt, who died before delivering this speech for a Jefferson Day broadcast in 1945. Only thoughts of peace can eradicate the beginnings of war. The dominant thinking in international politics is not yet based on a policy of peace creation. NATO, for instance, is not a creator or even a keeper of the peace. It merely manages the effects of a war mentality.

Only a new political sensibility arising throughout the world can counter the war machine always lurking in the background of international politics. Perhaps we will become bold enough to create what kind of world we want, instead of always trying to accomplish small gains within a system we know is ultimately destructive.

Traveling in India with a group of fellow Americans, I spent quite a bit of time in meditation and prayer near the Taj Mahal. There is a mosque right next to the Taj, and all true houses of worship, of whatever religion, hold spiritual power for people of faith. We had already found that, while we were meditating, Indian people would frequently come and join us, sit down in the group, and start meditating with us as though it was the most natural thing in the world. One particular day, as we came out of a deep period of silence, a line of about thirty or so Indians stood at the edge of the patio where we sat. We stood as if in a trance and faced our Indian counterparts. What followed in a sublime silence was an exchange of mutual honor and respect that was almost mind-altering. All of us were profoundly moved.

In a meeting with His Holiness the Dalai Lama, I learned some things about foreign policy. His Holiness told me that a German physicist had said to him that we should remove the concept of "foreign policy" from our minds and think of all nations as our "domestic partners."

We shouldn't be overimpressed by terms like "foreign policy," huge secretive counterintelligence agencies, and government departments that play the world like a giant chessboard and view it as no more than a game we're trying to win. *Our* consciousness should drive *them,* and not the other way around.

According to the esoteric wisdom of the ages, every nation

carries with it a facet of divine light as it streams from the Mind of God to earth. The soulful function associated with the United States is to "light the way."

America needs to reclaim our own inner light. "The people of the world," the Dalai Lama told me, "no longer look at America as a champion of democracy. Too many times we have seen you take the side of undemocratic forces." We are known as the great underminer of communism, to be sure, but that is far from synonymous with being a champion of freedom. We have sabotaged democratic governments as well as communist governments when they did not move in the direction we wanted them to move, and even today we sell out oppressed democratic forces for a greater market share of their country's economies.

In our international relations, we have become in most ways just like any other world player, seeking political and economic advantage, manipulating events according to what some would call our "vital national interests," though those interests today seem clearly defined more by economics than by values.

And what if we, the American people, were to *change our minds* about that? We shouldn't underestimate our power. The entire world would shift.

ANOTHER interesting thing happened to me at the Taj Mahal. The Mufti—Egypt's highest Muslim cleric—was visiting Agra at the time, and happened to pass our group as he walked through the area with his entourage. Seeing a group of Westerners meditating at the Taj Mahal made him curious, and he asked who we were. Upon being told we were a group of Christians and Jews from the United States, many of us clergy, he asked if he could meet with a small group of us later at his hotel.

The meeting was very formal and the Mufti spoke through an interpreter. His basic message to us was this: "I am aware that for most Americans, when you hear the word *Islamic*, you usually hear the word *terrorist* in the same sentence. I wanted to speak with you to make sure you understand that Islam is a religion of peace.

"Every people has a dark element—a group which does not represent the larger group well. Obviously, we have ours. But please do not think that Islamic terrorists represent true Islam, any more than Christians who commit violence in the name of God represent true Christianity, or Jews who commit violence in the name of God represent true Judaism."

After meeting with the Mufti, as I made my way through the lobby of the hotel, one of the Egyptians who was attending His Eminence tapped me on the shoulder and asked if we could speak. In the most gentle, gracious tones, he said that he wanted to tell me something.

During the very week that we were in India, a group of Indian women threatened to burn themselves alive in protest of the Miss Universe pageant being held in New Delhi. What they were protesting was the imposition of Western standards of beauty on Indian women, expressing the resentment that many Indians— indeed, many people throughout the Third World—feel toward America.

The Egyptian diplomat whom I met in the lobby of the hotel in Agra said to me,

I do not mean this as a criticism of the United States. I know the Americans are good men and women. But please try to make them understand: many people in my part of the world feel that they have been forced to try to keep up with you, in a race that we do not really care to run. Your technology is amazing, but America seems spiritually polluted to many of us. Your ways are not our ways, and while we were tempted for a while to think that your ways should be our ways, we do not think that anymore.

———

This is the problem, Ms. Williamson, and there will be terrible consequences in the world if Americans do not come to understand this. Islamic terrorists have had such success—if you can call their campaigns a success—because they have been able to persuade millions of peasants that America is bad. It was not too difficult to do, Ms. Williamson. All they have to do is describe the television programs you export to this part of the world, and millions of our people are very horrified.

Your government does not understand. They do not see how the people feel. We need the American people to understand. Perhaps you will bring more Americans to our part of the world. If they come to understand us, then they will respect us. We would feel that respect, and then I don't think that the terrorists would have such success. This is not a job the CIA can do. It is only a job which people can do.

I thanked him for telling me those things, and I promised him I would pass the information along.

AMERICA is not now the home of the brave, but I think we are the home of those who wish to be brave.

Coming back from Cairo to JFK Airport at the beginning of 1997, I handed my landing card to the agent at the U.S. Customs counter. He read what I had written.

"What do you do?" he asked me.

"I'm a writer," I replied.

"What do you write?"

"I'm writing a book about healing America."

He looked at me. "Well, America is *shot*," he said. I didn't say anything.

"You ought to come here for a day, to do research for your book. Come see what I see. These people are terrible."

I was rather shocked. "Do you mean immigrants?"

"Well," he hesitated, "Americans are the worst. But they're all bad. I came here wanting to like everybody, you know, thinking everybody's fairly decent. But immigrants now aren't like the immigrants fifty years ago. They might be good when they first come here, but after being around Americans for a couple of months, they're just as bad as we are."

I thought for a few moments, then ventured a comment. "Well, I have an idea that might help."

"Really?" he asked.

"When people come up to you here, look them in the eye and silently say, 'The goodness in me salutes the goodness in you.'"

He thought for a moment. "Would that maybe really work, you think?"

"Oh, yes," I said. "Really, it does."

He smiled and collected my card, showing me which way to exit.

As I reached the door leading out, I looked back at the agent. He was looking at me. We both stood still for a moment, in silence, our eyes locked.

The ancient Egyptians believed the stars in our eyes are reflections of the stars in the sky, and that the stars in the sky are our home. I had heard that in Egypt, but I learned it's true in America. I saw the stars in my brother's eyes, and I knew that I was home.

Appendix

THE GLOBAL RENAISSANCE ALLIANCE

If you are interested in ways to take part in the mystical revolution of American political consciousness, contact the Global Renaissance Alliance U.S.A.

Founded by myself and author Neale Donald Walsch, the Alliance provides every citizen the opportunity to engage democracy with soulfulness and love. Our national network of Citizen Circles is an exciting field of political possibility, and we hope you'll join our efforts to turn harmony, cooperation, sharing, and reverence for Life into dominant political values.

THE GLOBAL RENAISSANCE ALLIANCE
P.O. Box 15712
Washington, D.C. 20003
tel: 202-544-1219
fax: 202-347-0544
e-mail address: office@renaissancealliance.org
Web site: www.renaissancealliance.org

Suggested Reading

Bernstein, Richard B. with Kym S. Rice. *Are We to Be a Nation? The Making of the Constitution.* Cambridge, MA: Harvard University Press, 1987.

Boorstin, Daniel J. *The Americans,* 3 vol. New York: Random House, 1958–1973.

Brown, Jerry. *Dialogues.* Berkeley, CA: Berkeley Hills Books, 1998.

Carey, Ken. *Third Millennium.* San Francisco: Harper San Francisco, 1996.

Donald, David Herbert. *Lincoln.* New York: Simon & Schuster, 1995.

Elgin, Duane. *Awakening Earth.* New York: Morrow, 1993.

Gandhi, M. K. *An Autobiography or The Story of My Experiments with Truth.* London: Penguin Books, 1927.

Goldsmith, James. *The Trap.* New York: Carroll & Graf, 1994.

Gordon, James S. *Manifesto for a New Medicine.* New York: Addison-Wesley Publishing Company, Inc., 1996.

Guthman, Edwin O., and C. Richard Allen, eds. *RFK: Collected Speeches.* New York: Viking, 1993.

Hartmann, Thom. *The Last Hours of Ancient Sunlight: Waking Up to Personal and Global Transformation.* Northfield, VT: Mythical Books, 1998.

Hawken, Paul. *The Ecology of Commerce: A Declaration of Sustainability.* New York: Harper Business, 1993.

Heftel, Cecil. *End Legalized Bribery.* Washington, D.C.: Seven Locks Press, 1998.

Henderson, Hazel. *Building a Win-Win World: Life Beyond Global Economic Warfare.* San Francisco: Berrett-Koehler Publishers, 1996.

Houston, Jean. *A Mythical Life.* San Francisco: Harper San Francisco, 1997.

Houston, Jean. *Public Like a Frog: Entering the Lives of Three Great Americans.* Wheaton, IL: Quest Books, 1993.

Hubbard, Barbara Marx. *Conscious Evolution: Awakening the Power of Our Social Potential.* San Rafael, CA: New World Library, 1998.

Iyer, Raghavan. *The Essential Writings of Mahatma Gandhi.* Delhi: Oxford University Press, 1991.

Jefferson, Thomas. *Writings.* Ed. Merrill D. Peterson. New York: Library of America, 1984.

King, Martin Luther, Jr. *Testament of Hope: The Essential Writings and Speeches of Martin Luther King, Jr.* Ed. James M. Washington. San Francisco: Harper San Francisco, 1991.

Korten, David. *When Corporations Rule the World.* West Hartford, CT: Kumarian Press; San Francisco: Berrett-Koehler; 1995.

Lerner, Michael. *The Politics of Meaning: Restoring Hope and Possibility in an Age of Cynicism.* Malibu, CA: Perseus Press, 1996.

Lincoln, Abraham. *Speeches and Writings,* 2 vol. Ed. Don E. Fehrenbacher. New York: The Library of America, 1989.

McCaughlin, Corrinne and Gordon Davidson. *Spiritual Politics.* New York: Ballantine Books, 1994.

Oates, Stephen B. *Let the Trumpet Sound: The Life of Martin Luther King, Jr.* New York: Harper & Row, 1982.

Paine, Thomas. *Writings.* Ed. Eric Foner. New York: Library of America, 1995.

Reich, Robert. *Locked in the Cabinet.* New York: Alfred A. Knopf, 1997.

Rifkin, Jeremy. *The End of Work: The Decline of the Global Labor Force and the Dawn of the Post-Market Era.* New York: G. P. Putnam's Sons, 1995.

Roth, Robert. *The Natural Law Party: A Reason to Vote.* New York: St. Martin's Press, 1998.

Schechter, Stephen L., Richard B. Bernstein, and Donald S. Lutz, eds. *Roots of the Republic.* Madison, WI: Madison House, 1990.

Secretan, Lance H. K. *Reclaiming Higher Ground.* New York: McGraw-Hill, 1997.

Slater, Phillip. *A Dream Deferred: America's Discontent and the Search for a New Democratic Ideal.* Boston: Beacon Press, 1991.

Smith, Hedrick. *Rethinking America.* New York: Random House, 1995.

Smith, Huston. *The World's Religions.* San Francisco: Harper San Francisco, 1991.

Spence, Gerry. *Give Me Liberty: Freeing Ourselves in the Twenty-first Century.* New York: St. Martin's Press, 1998.

Tarnas, Richard. *The Passion of the Western Mind: Understanding the Ideas That Have Shaped Our World View.* New York: Ballantine Books, 1991.

Thurman, Robert. *Inner Revolution: Life, Liberty, and the Pursuit of Real Happiness.* New York: Riverhead Books, 1998.

Walsch, Neale Donald. *Conversations with God: An Uncommon Dialogue: Book 1.* New York: Putnam Publishing Group, 1996.

————. *Conversations with God: An Uncommon Dialogue: Book 2.* Charlottesville, VA: Hampton Roads, 1997.

————. *Conversations with God: An Uncommon Dialogue: Book 3.* Charlottesville, VA: Hampton Roads, 1998.

Washington, George. *Writings.* Ed. John Rhodehamel. New York: The Library of America, 1997.

Acknowledgments

Many people supported my efforts to rewrite this book. I am extremely grateful to Caroline Sutton at Simon & Schuster, plus the following friends and associates who paved the way for me to do so.

To Al Lowman, I am deeply grateful for literary midwifery of the highest order.

To Thom Hartmann, many thanks for help with the manuscript.

To Neale Donald Walsch and Jean Houston, many thanks for kind and generous support.

Many thanks to Charlotte Patton and B. G. Dillworth for most excellent and generous help. To my friends and associates Sandy Scott, Ann-Marie Wilk, Alan Semonian, Kathy Kalil, Mary Ellen Bushy, Linda Puryear, Charlette Manning, and many friends at the Church of Today, my thanks for carrying so much of my world for me while I attended to this one.

To Emma, who is the cutest and the sweetest, you are Mommy's favorite everything. Thank you for being such a perfect you.

To my mother, my deepest thanks for your constancy and love.

Index